Get over it!

SURVIVING GRIEF TO LIVE AGAIN

BY AUDREY STRINGER

GET OVER IT!:
Surviving Grief To Live Again

Copyright © 2005 Audrey Stringer

Edited and coordinated by FINA SCROPPO
Design, layout and production: MATTHEWS COMMUNICATIONS DESIGN INC.
Cover design: SHARON MATTHEWS
Contributing editor: LIZA FINLAY
Proofreader: HELEN KEELER

Library and Archives Canada Cataloguing in Publication

Stringer, Audrey, 1950-
Get over it! : surviving grief to live again / Audrey Stringer.

ISBN 0-9737132-0-8

1. Bereavement—Psychological aspects. I. Title.

BF724.85.G73S87 2005   155.9'37   C2005-902248-5

Published by A String of Hope Inc.
All inquiries should be addressed to: Audrey Stringer, A String of Hope Inc.,
P.O. Box 22037, Sarnia, ON N7S 6J4

Printed in Canada

CONTENTS

DEDICATION

I dedicate this book to my three beautiful grandchildren: Lyndsay, Tristan and McKinley. Their young lives have been filled with the loss of many loved ones and, through their grief journey, they have given me enormous strength and courage, as well as love, laughter and joy. I also dedicate this book to the memory of my husband, Rhod, my son Steven, my granddaughter Tate, my mom and all those special people who have touched my life and will remain forever in my memory and heart.

ACKNOWLEDGEMENTS

First of all, I would like to thank Nada and Bernadette for their support and faith in me by buying the first two copies of my book when it was just a rough, unseen manuscript two years ago.

My heartfelt thanks to my children: my son Gavin and daughter-in-law, June, and my daughter, Lexine, and son-in-law, Tim, for their love, support and enthusiasm throughout this book project. A warm thank you to my mom (posthumously) and my dad, whose love and support I cherish.

A special thank you to Brian for his love and support.

I'm so blessed to have so many wonderful extended family members and friends in my life who've walked with me on my journey. You know who you are and my heartfelt thanks to all of you.

To my clients over the years, thank you for allowing me to walk with you on your journey and for giving me the courage to share my story.

I also want to thank the educational mentors on my journey: Rabbi Earl Grollman, Sister St. John, Dr. Alan Wolfelt, Dr. Norman King. Thanks to Greta and Janet Podleski, who inspired me with their story of self-publishing, and to best-selling author David Chilton (*The Wealthy Barber*), who gave me the name of a brilliant editor and book designer.

My heartfelt thanks to my editor, Fina Scroppo, who did a superb job of editing this book.

I want to thank Sharon and Peter Matthews for their fantastic artistic cover design and layout.

INTRODUCTION

There were three main reasons I wanted to write this book. Number one was to help me cope with and survive my losses over the last few years. Number two was to help you, the bereaved, by creating a resource-filled tool. Third was to help those who may be supporting a friend or family member with his or her grief.

We will all die one day. Learning about grief and the mourning process will give you a sense of control and a feeling of normalcy when a loved one dies. Learning to take your pain and channel it into something positive will give you new purpose in life. I don't promise to have all the answers to help you cope with your grief, but I hope my bereavement journey will help you start the healing process.

All of us, in some way, have experienced losses or endings, from something as typical as the end of summer vacation, moving away from a familiar neighbourhood or confronting the prospect of retirement, to the death of a pet, friend or loved one. Whether losses are big or small, they're real to us. The more we value an experience or a person, the greater our reaction to loss. Grief is a normal reaction to loss, but if grief is repressed, it can lead to chronic physical and emotional problems. So, we need to deal with grief and its associated emotions, always keeping in mind that for healing to take place, you have to mourn (go public with your grief) by sharing your story over and over until you are able to integrate your loss into your everyday life.

My son Steven, my granddaughter Tate, and my husband, Rhod, died within seven years of each other. I was dealing with multiple, significant losses in a short time frame and never properly mourned their deaths until Rhod died. By this time, I was overwhelmed with grief and could not function emotionally, physically or spiritually. I was now forced to grieve and mourn all of them at the same time. There were days when it took every ounce of my strength to live each and every day.

I knew that I had to take charge of my life and make some changes. I was good at helping others but I was not good at letting others help me. It didn't help that people expected that I could cope better with my loved ones' deaths because I had been through it a number of times and that I was told I was the "expert," having worked in palliative care at the time. But who wants to be an expert in losing their loved ones?!

Thus began my long journey to finding hope. I had already begun taking grief counselling courses just after Steven died and while working in palliative care for years. After Rhod's death, I was determined to continue my additional training and education, take early retirement from my job and start my own grief counselling practice. I also began my path to healing by writing in my journal every day, which is why you'll see many journal entries from 1999. I wrote in my journals (four in total) for two years and then used them to develop a plan to write this book. But I wasn't able to re-read my journals again for another six months because I did not have the courage to face my pain. Just when I had completed my rough manuscript, on December 25, 2002, my beloved grandmother Avery (my mother's mother) died at age 99. I felt sad because I was going to miss regular visits with her and our birthday celebrations (our birthdays took place in the same week), but I was at peace with her death.

In the process of developing this book, I experienced three more significant losses within a few weeks of each other. My dear mother died suddenly on November 27, 2003, my Aunt Prissie the following week and my brother-in-law, Walter, two weeks later. I thought I had lost all the incentive to finish my book, but I took a few months off and my loved ones' spirits spurred me on. There was a special moment that gave me more reassurance that I needed to complete this book. When my grieving 85-year-old father visited me last summer, I was so afraid that he would die before I published my book that I asked him to read one of my rough chapters, "Building A Supportive Network." He sat and read it at the kitchen table and I left the room. When I came back, Dad was wiping the tears from his eyes and said, "Audrey, you're going to help so many people with this book." I knew he was right, so I was even more determined than ever to finish it. I could also hear my mother's voice telling me, "Finish it. Get over it, get on with it, girl!"

One of my biggest decisions was coming up with a book title that was representative of my message. When I first considered the book title *Get Over It!*, I thought it was too harsh. I remember feeling hurt and angry when people often asked me, "Are you over your grief yet?" But I later realized that I did get over the intense pain of my loss and was able to live my life again, even though I was a changed person. I also realized that "getting over" grief does not mean you are forgetting your loved one; it means you'll need to get over the intense pain of losing someone in your own time and with a healthy support network. Getting over it means you'll need to get over the scars that grief has left with you and rebuild a new life with new hopes and dreams, even though you can't see it right now.

My challenge, then, became to live a new life, independent of the loved ones that had died. I had to rediscover who I was and who I wanted to be. Today, despite my losses, I am living life to the fullest, and I have a successful grief counselling practice, as well as a yoga teaching business. It's a time of moving on for me and I now consider myself a survivor of grief rather than its victim.

As you read this book and explore my grief journey, I hope you gain the strength and courage to deal with your pain and realize that you are not alone. Before you get over the pain of loss, you will need to befriend it and make it a part of you. Only then, can you let it go and get on with your life.

God bless you.

LOOKING BACK

As I look back over the past 12 years, I feel a deep sense of pride in myself. Despite the death of loved ones, I 'survived' my losses. But I had to work hard throughout these years to get to this point. Here's the story of how my loved ones died and the events that prompted me to write this book.

My son Steven died on August 25, 1992, my granddaughter Tate on September 12, 1994, and my husband, Rhod, on February 6, 1999. While I was writing this book, several other family members, including my beloved mother and grandmother, left this life. My son and daughter-in-law also experienced three miscarriages.

I will never forget that dreadful phone call that awakened me from a deep sleep a few minutes after 1 a.m. on August 26, 1992. It changed my life forever. When I picked up the phone, I heard the words "Steven jumped off the Bluewater Bridge!" Naturally, I was stunned and yelled back, "Is this a bad joke!" and hung up. I later learned it was Gabrielle, my daughter-in-law who had been recently separated from Steven, who was calling. Just as I told Rhod what happened, the phone rang again and he picked it up – on the other end was a police officer verifying the information. Within minutes, two police officers were at the front door to tell us that Steven had driven his truck to the Bluewater Bridge in Point Edward (connecting Canada to the

United States), had gotten out and was seen jumping off. The rescue teams from Sarnia and Port Huron began their search for Steven's body in the early morning hours and, by late afternoon, found Steven's lifeless body in the Sarnia harbour. It was the longest 16 hours that my family and I have ever experienced. Buoy 68 became his temporary resting place – a piece of his clothing had attached itself to the buoy. Ironically, Steven was born in 1968.

On September 12, 1994, my second grandchild was to be born. My daughter, Lexine, was two weeks overdue and her physician expected her to deliver a big baby, so she scheduled her delivery for the morning of September 12. We were all excited and looking forward to seeing the new baby. For more than nine months we had called the baby Tate, the name Lexine and her husband, Tim, had decided to call their child whether it was a boy or girl, named after Steven's middle name.

But something went wrong shortly after Lexine's inducement. Lexine was hemorrhaging and the medical staff did an emergency C-section. Tate came into this world weighing more than 10 pounds but she was in distress. Lexine was hemorrhaging but it was Tate's blood that drained from her body. Tate was immediately placed on life support, but she didn't make it through the day. We were all in shock. We were planning another funeral so soon after Steven's death. Tate was buried with her uncle Steven at the foot of his plot at Lakeview Cemetery and Crematorium.

Six years after Steven's death and four years after Tate's death, life at the Stringers was starting to feel joyful again but I was not prepared for what was going to happen on January 5, 1999. Rhod and I had always taken a Caribbean vacation after Christmas day and 1998 was no exception. We decided last minute to go to Tampico, Mexico, for a fun-filled week.

We returned to Toronto, Ontario, where we stayed in a hotel overnight before our three-hour drive home to Sarnia. The weather was stormy and the roads were slippery, but Rhod was comfortable driving. About halfway into our drive, Rhod suddenly felt intense pain in his lower back and told me that I would have to drive the remainder of the trip home. I insisted that we head for the local hospital, but Rhod refused, so we compromised on staying at a nearby hotel for the night. But minutes after midnight, Rhod's condition was worsening and I gave him the choice of either taking an ambulance or a cab to the hospital. He opted for the cab and now I was really scared. We spent the rest of the early morning in emergency; by now, Rhod was going into kidney failure and within 24 hours, he experienced three organ failures – kidneys, lungs and pancreas – and was in an induced coma.

Our final words to each other were "I love you" before Rhod slipped into a coma, where he remained unresponsive for the next 30 days before life support was disconnected.

MOVING FORWARD

Despite losing three significant family members within seven years, I was able to get over the intense pain of my losses. The number-one factor in my healing was the decision to find healthy ways to do so.

As I reflect on my past, I feel I had two choices. One was to curl on my bed and sink into a deep depression, or to pick myself up and work on every emotion I had during my bereavement journey. I chose the latter.

I looked to my childhood, which was built on a strong foundation, and my support network for inspiration and it filled me with faith and hope as I began my journey. It has been painful and joyful at the same time, and I have no regrets. In the last few years, I have opened my own grief counselling practice, take care of myself by teaching yoga and eating a healthy diet, and have even found love again.

This journey has opened my eyes and eased my fear of dying. There is something worse than death and that is being afraid to live. The year that Rhod died, a co-worker of mine named Vonda gave me an angel pin and a card with the Latin words "*carpe diem*" in it. These words mean "seize the day" and that is how I live my life today because tomorrow may never come. So I don't dwell on the yesterdays because they are gone and I don't waste today, but I live as if it were my very last day alive.

CHAPTER 1

COPING
WITH DEATH

My view of the world changed when my son Steven died. It changed again when my granddaughter Tate died and again when my husband, Rhod, died. How was I going to cope with all of these significant losses? I found it even more difficult to cope because of people's expectations. I was working in the palliative care field at the time, so family, friends and peers expected me to be strong, get over my grief quickly and move on with life.

I was good at giving support, but not good at receiving it. Now I had to learn to reach out to others to help me cope. After all, I was human just like them.

To mourn well is to live well and you will have to find what works for you. Your grief journey is yours and yours alone. It's a unique experience that will depend on your personality, cultural heritage, relationship with your loved one and the circumstances of the death. Here's my story of how I coped.

MY STORY

COPING WITH THREE LOSSES

When I first learned about my son Steven's death, I remember feeling as if someone had kicked me in the stomach and knocked me to my knees. The physical and emotional pain was unbearable, and I began to question my faith.

I nitially, I experienced numbness, tightness in my throat and chest, loss of control of my bladder and bowels. I was in shock and it lasted for several months. When the shock wore off, the pain of his loss became more intense. Now, I was overwhelmed with sadness, tears and guilt, and I yearned to have him back. I missed his presence, his phone calls, visits, gentleness and beautiful smile. Sometimes the void was unbearable, but I was thankful that we had a big part of him in our life – his 18-month-old daughter, Lyndsay. When I saw her, she gave me hope and joy. Still, even a year after Steven's death my emotions were extreme, ranging from sadness to joy to anger to a feeling of emptiness.

The wound in my heart and soul from Steven's death was still open when my newborn granddaughter Tate died two years later. I couldn't believe this was happening again to our family. I experienced the same physical and emotional symptoms as when Steven died, but now I hurt for my daughter, Lexine, and I felt helpless because I couldn't take away her pain. I had so many 'why?' questions, but found no answers. I was searching for meaning in my life, a natural reaction when a loved one dies.

In an unexpected twist, Tate's death helped me to better cope with Steven's death. Now, my daughter and I had a bond because of our children's deaths and our relationship became very special. We worried about each other and leaned on each other for support. Over time, I found solace in believing that Tate was with Steven and he was looking after her. This gave me immense hope in my dark hours and my broken heart began to heal. I knew it was a matter of time before my wound would completely heal and I'd be left only with a scar as a reminder of my losses.

Realize that you never truly get over grief.

Once you decide to make grief your friend, you'll live well. Check with your funeral director, surf the Internet or check your local library for resources for bereaved people (see our Resources section, page 209, for more information). I've been fortunate to focus my work and studies on the grief and bereavement processes, as well as to have walked with many wonderful people on their journeys – without this experience, my journey would have been very different. You'll need to understand your personality and apply what has helped you cope in the past to your present loss.

Being the Caregiver

MY WOUND WAS RIPPED OPEN AGAIN WHEN MY HUSBAND, Rhod, died less than five years later. In my heart, I knew he was dying during his 30 days in the hospital, but I wasn't prepared for the finality of his death.

Throughout his hospital stay, I looked after everyone – my family, friends and even family members of people I came to befriend at the hospital. I was my own social worker and theirs too. In other words, I coped by being everyone else's caregiver.

I was high on adrenaline, focusing my energies on getting Rhod's doctors to discontinue his life support instead of dealing with my own well-being. I struggled with the many procedures doctors performed on Rhod that seemed fruitless and experimental. When I finally let

Rhod go, I felt a sense of relief, but that relief was accompanied by immense pain. Now I had little to fight for and I found myself totally exhausted, as if I was in a drugged state. I prayed to God for the strength to organize Rhod's funeral and be there for my family. My heart was totally shattered and I wondered how I was going to survive.

I questioned my faith over and over, but I finally realized that God is a loving God. After Rhod died, I enrolled in several bible study courses to help me find the meaning to go on. I also found comfort in my church community. Only then was I able to find peace and solace.

Nourish your soul, mind and body.

I believe in a higher power and this has been a strong source of strength for me. I prayed to God to give me the strength to get through one moment, one hour and sometimes one day. Our Gods may be different, but you can seek whatever spiritual source gives you strength. Nourish your mind with positive thoughts of family, friends and good health.

COPING WITH FUNERALS

I WENT THROUGH A SERIES OF EMOTIONS AND ROLES during the three funerals of my family members – from organizer and planner to distraught mother/grandmother to strong and stoic wife. But no matter how I coped, I came crashing down at the end of each funeral.

DEALING WITH ANGER

Anger, which can be expressed outwardly or inwardly, is common during this time. It's often targeted at the deceased loved one or God. If emotions are repressed, anger can take its toll on self-esteem and physical and mental health. In severe circumstances, it can lead to chronic feelings of guilt, depression and possibly suicide. The grieving person may feel agitated, tense and restless.

In a healthy grief journey, a person's emotions need to be expressed, not repressed. Find a supportive friend who will validate your feelings and let you express them.

Ironically, one of the biggest aids in planning Steven's funeral was to keep telling myself that it wasn't really happening. Thank God for denial! This was somebody else's family and I was just helping out. Even when I realized that it wasn't a dream, I got the strength to go on from the many people who came to Steven's visitation – some who shared their stories about Steven with me; others who told me they admired my strength. If enough people tell you you're a pillar of strength, then you believe them! But the danger is that you stop caring for yourself – you're convinced

Cry, cry, cry.

Free those tears. The people in your life may not like to see you cry because they feel helpless. Find someone you can trust to let you cry as much and for as long as you need. Remember to drink lots of water to replenish those tears. Crying is exhausting, but it's sometimes necessary to cope with your loss. I cried so much the first 18 months after Rhod's death that I thought there were no more tears left inside me.

that you need to take care of everyone else around you. I intellectualized Steven's death, but didn't truly accept the loss until six years later.

Sometimes, demonstrating strength gives people the wrong impression and I had to cope with that experience at Rhod's funeral. I organized and planned my husband's funeral with precision and clarity. I wanted to celebrate Rhod's life, but I also knew that such a ceremony would facilitate my grieving process. Throughout the visitation and funeral, I was in a robot-like state. I compare my actions to Jackie Kennedy – who portrayed a strong and brave exterior when thanking everyone with a

Laughter is the best medicine for healing a hurting spirit.

You may feel guilty when you laugh and feel happy, but you should treasure these moments. Surround yourself with positive, nurturing people or watch a funny movie in the company of friends. Don't be afraid to take a happy break. It's also okay to cry and laugh at the same time.

smile – yet I kept all my emotions locked inside me. I felt as if I was going to crumble and crack like a cement wall.

Several people told me that they thought I was strong because I had been through this before. "It must get easier after each loss," they commented. But, they couldn't have been more mistaken. I never responded to these remarks, but I wanted to scream and yell, "You have no idea what I'm feeling at this time and I pray to God that you never have to!"

Another well-meaning person asked me if it was easier to lose my child or my husband. She answered her own question when she said, " I think it would be your child because you can't replace your child, but you can replace your husband." I felt sad for her ignorance, and God gave me the strength to forgive her.

Making Arrangements

PLANNING THE DETAILS OF A LOVED ONE'S FUNERAL can help you confront your grief. For Steven, we had a big church funeral even though he died of suicide. I celebrated his life with pride and honour. I didn't want to restrict his funeral to family as so many do when a family member takes his own life; they can't deal with the stigma attached to suicide and, in essence, they send a message to the community that they don't need their support. Instead, I wanted my community to know that we needed extra support to cope with our loss.

Reaching Out

If you can't express your feelings with a trustworthy friend, try finding refuge by writing them in a journal or seeking counselling. Contact your local mental health association, funeral director or family physician for referrals.

Tate's funeral service was held in the hospital chapel because my daughter, Lexine, was still hospitalized. The pastoral care team was very supportive and kind. Tate wore my children's baptismal gown and was buried with Steven at the foot of his grave plot, which gave all of us much comfort.

What was different for me this time was that I now had to cope with a whole new set of feelings; aside from the deep sadness, confusion and helplessness, my heart was breaking for my daughter and son-in-law, whose daughter died before they could enjoy her. I knew their hopes and dreams were shattered.

Find a cause to fuel your energies.

Helping others will help you take your mind off yourself. You may want to make a career change, pursue a new hobby or even start a support group for the bereaved. I was working with clients who were dying and bereaved; I found it life-giving and it gave me a sense of purpose and worth.

Being Alone

AS HARD AS IT WAS TO BURY MY LOVED ONES, IT WAS the time period following the funerals that tested my ability to cope the most. I remember, particularly after Rhod's funeral, that I didn't want to be caregiver and organizer to my family anymore. Rhod's death took away my need to take care of everybody, to try to do the right things and worry about what other people thought of me. I was relieved when family from out of town left my home one week later – I didn't want to talk to anyone or see anyone. I needed to be alone with my grief.

Be gentle with yourself.

Each day will be different. The first year after your loss may be difficult, and sometimes the second year is even more difficult. Society will try to rush you through your mourning process but your grief is yours and yours alone, so take your time. If you have loved hard, you'll grieve hard. Getting through the process faster won't make it any better.

Journaling

FOR A COUPLE OF MONTHS, I EXPERIENCED MANY sleepless nights. When I closed my eyes, I saw Rhod and recalled all of the procedures he underwent and I would wake up in a sweat. I realized that before I was able to grieve and mourn I needed to deal with the trauma of his death. I needed to externalize my emotions because I had internalized them for the 30 days of his hospitalization. My only outlet was to write about the horrific 30 days in a journal. In the beginning, I was only able to write a few words each day, but over time I was able to finish this journal. It wasn't until three years after Rhod's death that I had the courage to read about his ordeal in the hospital in my journals. It was still painful and I was very vulnerable, but I needed to revisit this pain to get rid of some of the bitter feelings I felt toward the medical system. This process helped me find a little peace and put closure on this experience.

Coping with Work

I RETURNED TO WORK TWO WEEKS AFTER STEVEN'S death and spent the same amount of time at home after Tate died. I wasn't ready to return to work, especially after Steven's death, but Rhod thought that it would be good for both of us to resume our normal activities. For us, life was never going to be normal again, yet we wanted structure in our lives.

Learn to say "no" to well-meaning friends.

But it's equally important not to isolate yourself. Grief and mourning is hard work and you need the strength to go through this process. Listen to your body and don't feel guilty if you take a nap in the afternoon. Rest! Rest! Rest your mind, body and soul.

Rhod wanted to be 'doing' and I wanted to just exist. Sure, I could use the distraction, but looking back, I needed more time to come to terms with my loss and let my heart and soul wallow for a while in this pit of despair.

I was working two part-time positions with a not-for-profit health-care organization. It was hard enough finding the energy to perform my typical duties at work, but now I faced conflicting messages from my supervisors – one of whom was very supportive and the other who was anything but supportive.

Even among co-workers, I was met with mixed reactions. At one workplace, staff would greet me with hugs. I was thankful that I had a nurturing workplace at least three days a week. At my other job, however, co-workers often passed right by me in the hallways without looking at me. They did not know what to say or do. Many of them were mothers and I think my experience made them uncomfortable – they realized it could happen to them.

My department had a policy that volunteers could not work in palliative care and bereavement until one year after a loved one died. But, I was a paid staff person and I didn't expect to be slotted into the same category as a volunteer. I felt there was no reason why I couldn't separate my personal life from my working environment. I wanted to prove that I was 'professional,' and nobody was going to tell me that I couldn't do my job. To prove it, I assumed extra duties and continued with my studies, determined to complete my degree in sociology. I was strong. I could handle any challenge and no one was going to stop me. I loved my job and I wasn't going to be labelled as weak, at least not in front of my co-workers.

My stubborn nature and my fight to survive, however, prevented me from grieving properly. I hid my emotions at work, subconsciously scheduling my mourning time for when I went home. I did my crying in the car, on my way home from work and from my classes, and in bed at night. I needed to share my sadness, emptiness and loss – to be able to tell my story over and over again. Instead, I played the role of a mother who was a pillar of strength, and that was the message I was sending to my peers.

Rhod's death gave me no choice but to stay home. I could not function at work. I was physically, emotionally and spiritually drained. I was off work for four months. When I did return, it was for only three days a week. But that was short-lived and I decided to take early retirement on November 1, 2000. All I wanted to do was take each day at a time. Life is so short and I wanted to make the most of it. Today, I have no regrets with my decision.

Coping with Fear

I DIDN'T KNOW FEAR, THAT IS, REAL FEAR, UNTIL THE loss of my family members. Half of my immediate family had died and now I feared the loss of my other two children and grandchildren. This fear was so intense it would wake me at night. It stopped me from doing things, like going into town for the day. I was a more panicked mother to my daughter and son. I phoned them constantly to reassure myself that they were safe. I needed to tell them that I loved them more often. These were the last words that Rhod and I shared, but I never got a chance to tell Steven before he died.

My fear later turned to anger – anger at Steven for choosing to die and not thinking of those who were left behind to pick up the pieces. I often felt as if I had lost control of my life. I was angry with Rhod for leaving me. He was my anchor in the roughest storms and my greatest supporter.

NORMAL FEARS

Three losses in seven years left me with many fears. Coping with certain fears after a loss is normal, but over time they shouldn't prevent you from resuming normal activities and loving relationships. Here are just some of the fears I experienced:

FEAR of my other children dying

FEAR of my grandchildren dying

FEAR of being alone and not being loved again

FEAR of being alone in my home…that I may not be able to live alone now

FEAR of driving my car

FEAR of surviving my losses

FEAR of something being wrong with me…why did my loved ones die?

FEAR of my own death

FEAR of loss of security (The world has changed and you don't feel safe anymore.)

FEAR of abandonment

FEAR of loss of financial, job security

FEAR of relationships ending

Coping with Every Day

AFTER EACH LOSS, I WAS EMOTIONALLY AND PHYSICALLY exhausted. I went to bed tired and I struggled to get up in the mornings.

Many days were a blur. My concentration level was very limited and my memory was compromised. There were many days when I drove home from work, yet didn't remember the ride. That scared me. I also had a tendency to misplace my house or car keys or my purse. I once found my car keys in the fridge and I left stove burners on a couple of times. I missed scheduled appointments and forgot to pay bills. I would write a list and then forget where I placed it. Finally, I began to keep a to-do list in my daytimer and ticked off each task as it was completed. I was going through the motions of existing in this time frame. It took me about eight months to return to a somewhat normal state. I finally realized that it was useless sweating the small stuff – like losing my keys. Besides, the more agitated I became, the more I was unable to concentrate and focus on the things that really mattered.

From my experience, I learned some valuable lessons on coping, primarily that it's important to seek support from your family, peers and friends. Remember, you're not a failure if you seek professional support to deal with your loss. There are many support services in your community – from one-on-one counselling for those who prefer private sessions to bereavement support groups for those who are more comfortable in group settings. Being with others who are experiencing similar situations and talking about your story over and over again can be very helpful during your healing journey.

∼ From My Journal ∼

March 16, 1999 – I feel as if I am in a daze...this isn't real. Rhod isn't dead. Then I tell myself Rhod died on Feb. 6. I am trying to do one task today – one phone call to the bank and get the information that I need. It took me all morning to psyche myself up to make that phone call and now I am totally exhausted for the rest of the day. I have to lie down so I can get the energy to accomplish the next task tomorrow.

July 13, 1999 – I got a phone call from my mom. Josh (my brother-in-law) died this morning. He died of a brain tumour. I am glad that I am only working today and off for the next two days, otherwise I don't know how I will manage to cope. I am visiting a young man diagnosed with a brain tumour today. I pray to God to give me the strength to be present for him and to get through this day.

July 17, 1999 – Today I am feeling like I did yesterday – empty, lost, sad and so alone. At this point, I feel like all of my dreams and goals died with Rhod. I know deep within my heart and soul that I have to make new dreams and goals, but dammit, I can't right now. My patience and tolerance of people today is very limited. People complain about the most mundane things and I want to scream at them and tell them to appreciate what they have and to look at what I've lost. It's easier to say nothing and leave the room, so I do.

April 5, 2000 – I woke up this morning and I look forward to this new day. I'm questioning who I am now. Where do I belong? I can't answer these questions. I imagine that with time I won't be thinking about these questions as much. I gain hope from being present for others in their grief. They give me strength and courage as they share their journey with me. I feel comfortable with my aloneness now. I feel a new sense of confidence and my self-esteem is increasing. I understand this is a journey and that I must go through this process and that no one else can do it for me. I have made a plan. I tell myself not to worry about tomorrow because tomorrow isn't here yet. I tell myself not to worry about yesterday – yesterday is gone. Only deal with this day. I only have today.

May 10, 2003 – My plan to publish my journal is starting to unfold. This is a journey of hope that I want to share with others to assist them on their path of grief and mourning. I want to share that I now live a healthy, happy life and have grown emotionally and spiritually through my losses.

Strategies: Coping Methods

You'll need to choose whatever coping method works best for you.
Here's a list of some of the strategies that helped me cope with my losses.

1. KEEP A JOURNAL.

Writing in my journal was one of the most important methods of
emotional survival. I needed to take my intense feelings and
heartache from inside and bring them out. For me, putting them
on paper was cathartic. Besides, my journal did not judge me.

2. WELCOME MUSIC.

The power of music has a way of calming body, mind and soul. I
needed music to lower my anxiety level and soothe my mind,
especially while I rested. I enjoyed classical and opera, but you
can choose whatever sound you like for the same benefits.

3. TAKE PART IN YOGA OR RELAXATION EXERCISE.

I have practiced yoga for 25 years. Its combination of deep
breathing and flexible postures helps de-stress my mind and
body, as well as help me re-energize. I found walking healing,
too. You may prefer to jog, swim or hike – any exercise that will
energize you.

4. ENJOY THE BENEFITS OF MASSAGE THERAPY.

The power of touch is so important during this time. It not
only makes us feel comforted, but therapeutic massage helps

rid the body of harmful toxins and helps relieve tension in the body's stress points, such as the neck, shoulders and back.

5. DON'T DISCOUNT SELF-TALK.

Understandably, self-esteem is low during the grieving process. I had to constantly tell myself, yes, I could still do certain things. It's OK to have a blue day, but then get up and get going.

6. SOCIALIZE, DON'T ISOLATE.

I valued being around friends and family. Surround yourself with those who will let you tell your story over and over until you're able to integrate it within your heart and soul. Talk about your loved one and call him by name. Tell them that it's important you do this. Just don't wait for your friends to call you – call them and invite them over.

7. GET DIRTY IN THE GARDEN.

I found solace in my garden. My journey was enriched by digging in the soil, planting flowers and bulbs and seeing new life in the spring despite the bittersweet feelings it stirred within me.

8. ENJOY THE WONDERS OF MOTHER NATURE.

It's a powerful healer because it reminds us of the incredible wonder around us. I walked many miles in local parks and along rivers. I sat for hours gazing at butterflies and listening to the music of birds. I travelled to Alaska to see the majestic glaciers and peaceful lakes.

RESOURCES

1. *When Bad Things Happen to Good People* by Harold S. Kushner.
(Avon Books, 1981)
The author wrote this book after his 14-year-old son died. It's a life-affirming book that talks about the struggle with hard times and personal pain. It's filled with compassion and hope.

2. *The Road Less Travelled: A New Psychology of Love, Traditional Values and Spiritual Growth* by Scott M. Peck, MD (A Touchstone Book, 1978)
One of its main messages: suffering enables us to reach a greater level of self-understanding. The author draws his material from extensive experience as a practicing psychiatrist.

3. *Final Gifts: Understanding The Special Awareness, Needs and Communication of The Dying* by Maggie Callanan and Patricia Kelley (Poseidon Press, 1992; Bantam, 1993)
This is the true, intimate story of two hospice nurses working with terminal patients at the edge of life and the lessons these patients taught them, such as wisdom, faith and love. One of my volunteers read this book to help her journey with her mom as she was dying. It helped her immensely, and to commemorate her mom, she donated 15 of these books to a library for palliative/hospice volunteers to read.

4. *Embraced By the Light* by Betty J. Eadie and Curtis Taylor (Gold Leaf Press, 1992)
It helped me cope with Steven's and Rhod's deaths and taught me that there is life after death.

CHAPTER 2

THE VALUE
OF RITUALS

Our society is filled with rituals and ceremonies. We use them to mark the passages in our lives, including births and anniversaries. We use ritual and ceremony to recognize achievements, such as graduation, and observe religious traditions, such as baptism, confirmation and bar mitzvah. Even the opening game of the baseball season has the celebratory first pitch.

Rituals and symbols are often used when words are not enough to express our feelings, whether these feelings are pain or joy. We have funerals to honour our loved ones when they die, but this ritual also assists us in the grief journey; it helps us accept reality and to believe that our loved ones have died. But beyond the funeral rites, there are other rituals you can create for yourself to help the healing. Here is how I used the power of rituals and symbols to help my family, friends and myself come to terms with our losses.

SPECIAL MOMENTS TO TREASURE

When I grew up, we viewed death as being a natural part of the life cycle. We wore black arm bands to symbolize bereavement; we held lavish funerals to mark the passage of a life and wakes to celebrate the time the deceased spent with us.

It was natural for us to have an open casket and the body of the deceased was buried in the cemetery. Family members and close friends took on the role of pallbearers – a role of great honour. The family, with the support of other community members, dug the grave for the burial of the deceased and everyone was present at the graveside ceremony. Then family members and friends lowered the casket into the earth and shovelled the soil scoop by scoop until the casket was covered.

We videotaped my husband Rhod's funeral. I wanted the family members and friends who were unable to attend to have an opportunity to say goodbye through this ritual. It was also important for our family to have this record so that when my grandchildren were older, they had the option of viewing the tape if they wanted.

Surround yourself with mementos.

After Rhod died, many of my friends gave me angel pins. Several also gave me figurines and I have them displayed in my office. When I look at these angels I can feel my loved ones around me, as well as a sense of peace.

I still find comfort in the tradition of this burial rite. But there are other rituals, equally meaningful. Storytelling is one of them. I remember Dad and Mom regaling us with great stories about Grandfather Avery after he died. Somehow, hearing joyful tales of his life helped ease the loss – it gave relevance to his time on earth and made the passage somehow easier to accept. It wasn't immediate, but in the months after the death of my husband and son, hearing stories about their achievements, funny moments, even losses, helped – it kept their memory alive and at the time, that was soothing. Reliving these memories was particularly comforting when my son Steven died, at only 23 years old. It helped me understand that despite his short life, he had led a full life.

Decorating cemetery plots is a seemingly frivolous ritual that I find comforting, too. It helps me include my loved ones in important moments – to reconnect to their memory. At Christmas, for example,

Don't feel pressured to accept rituals you're not comfortable with.

It's important for you to find the rituals that will help you. When my friend Maria's son died, she did not want an open casket despite the family pressure for her to do so. She compromised and had an open casket for family only.

we place wreaths on Rhod's and Steven's graves and once, we even erected a small Christmas tree. In the spring, it helped me to plant flowers. The ritual of digging in the soil with my hands and planting and then watching these flowers grow over time gave me hope. When I looked at the flowers I reflected on Steven's life and I felt a connection with him that I wasn't willing to let go of.

Sometimes you'll have to stand firm on your choice of rituals and symbols. When our son Steven died, our other son Gavin was remembering when Steven occasionally enjoyed a

Include children in your rituals.

When the husband of one of my clients died, he was the beloved poppa of eight grand-children. During his funeral service, each child carried one of his favourite items and placed it beside the casket. One child carried his favourite ball cap, another his golf club and on and on until finally the two-year-old presented a banana – because Poppa liked bananas. My grandchildren created artwork and placed it in their Grandpa's casket.

cigar. During the first viewing, he tucked a cigar in Steven's jacket; however, Rhod's dad got upset and pulled the cigar out of the pocket. Rhod gently told his father that it was okay and placed the cigar back in Steven's pocket. The point is: be true to what YOU believe to be healing.

MAKING RITUALS PERSONAL

When my granddaughter Tate died, my friend Dorothy gave me a butterfly pin to wear on my lapel – the butterfly being a symbol of life and free flight. When my friend Carol's mom died, I passed it on to her to wear. That pin has since passed on from hand to hand and all those who've worn it have found the brooch, and the spirit it embodies, incredibly comforting. Is there an object or a symbol your loved one cherished that could be passed around to signify love, loss and, most importantly, life?

BORROWING FROM OTHER CULTURES

My neighbour and friend is **Islamic**. In her faith, the deceased are immediately washed, then their bodies wrapped in a white cloth. After the community gathers to perform the funeral prayer for the deceased, the body is buried facing Ka'ba, in the holy city of Mecca. For the next days, visitors pay their respect to the family. Although Muslims are expected to mourn for the deceased, excessive screaming and wailing are not allowed because one should mourn by showing increased devotion to God and realize God's mercy; in Islam, death means departure from this life, and the beginning of a wonderful next life. How comforting a thought.

In the **Jewish** faith, there is an official mourning period, called Shiva, of seven days in which mourners pay respects to the deceased and his or her family. But after one year, the grieving process must end – prayers are said and candles lit on the anniversary of the death, in part to symbolically mark the end of mourning and the beginning of life without the deceased. Those unable to leave the loved one behind are counselled by the rabbi and encouraged to let go in a communal, supportive intervention.

Native Canadians burn sacred plants, chant and drum or hold a pipe ceremony to send off the deceased in style. Rituals vary with the nation. A wake, to pay final respects, is also customary.

Buddhists believe that only the body dies – the spirit lives on in another form. So all rituals celebrate the possibility of rebirth in a higher form. In ancient Buddhist cultures, ashes were taken to a mountaintop and thrown skyward to release the soul to its next life and its higher purpose.

HELPING THE LIVING

You might want to start a new ritual that helps give meaning to a lost life. Why not start ritually donating to a cause that was meaningful to your loved one? I found that giving to others really helped the grieving process.

PLANNING TIPS

1. Don't rush the funeral.

Take time to plan rituals for funerals and include immediate family members. Rituals are important to facilitate your grief journey and to memorialize your loved one.

2. Examine what is customary in your ethnic background/geographic area.

You may have been born in one country but now live in another. Incorporate some of these past rituals with the present rituals.

3. Think about the legacy that your loved one left behind to help family members.

Involving family and friends in funeral rituals is very healing. For us, it was very meaningful for family and friends to take part in the service. My friend Jane played the piano; my daughter, Lexine, composed a poem and together with my son Gavin read it at their brother Steven's funeral.

4. Plan the funeral/memorial to reflect your spirituality or faith.

It's important to have a ceremony that reflects who you are and how your loved one lived. There is no ritual that is weird, silly or unnecessary. If you are traditional and want to add some personal touches that's okay, too.

❧ From My Journal ❧

April 6, 1999 – This is our wedding anniversary and I sit reviewing our life together and then I think about Rhod's funeral. I review the rituals. The memory boards filled with photos. The many stories of Rhod that people shared with me. It was very difficult and draining for me, but I wouldn't change anything.

February 6, 2000 – One year ago today since Rhod died. Lexine and I are in St. Maarten for one week. I decided to go away around the anniversary of Rhod's death, but I still remember in detail his death and the funeral. I am reliving every second and it was as if it were today. I go over it in my mind as I am sitting here on the sandy beach bathing in the sunshine. I think about the visitations, the church service and the cemetery. I feel very sad but am happy that so much ritual was involved because it did help us on our grief journey.

Strategies: Creating Rituals

We can borrow rituals from other cultures or create new ones. Here are a few you may want to practice.

1. THE RITUAL OF PRAYER.

For me prayer was beneficial in my healing journey. When I was feeling low I would pray to my God to give me strength and courage to get through each moment, each hour, and each day.

2. BURN A LETTER.

It is may be helpful to write a letter to your loved one. You may not have the opportunity to say goodbye before the death and want to express your feelings in this way. For example, one of my clients lost her husband in a car crash and she felt guilty because their last communication had been an angry fight. She wrote a loving, apology letter and then burned it.

3. WEAR YOUR HEART ON YOUR SLEEVE.

Find a comforting symbol and wear it. When people ask you about this symbol you can tell them the story of your loss and how this object keeps your loved one's memory alive. I wore a butterfly pin that my friend Dorothy gave me. Maybe you have a T-shirt or baseball cap with warming words. "I wear this in honour of my mother/son/spouse, who died on November 27, 2003."

4. CREATE A MEMORIAL FOREST.

Planting trees in memory of loved ones is not only helpful in our grief and mourning journey, it is also good for the environment. This ritual, which we've adopted in our family, has helped my family mourn the loss of our loved ones. I don't feel so alone in my grief when I walk in the forest.

5. MAKE A SPECIAL MARKER FOR THE GRAVESITE.

Planning Rhod's marker at the cemetery helped me mourn. I chose a boulder because he liked rocks and stones. He loved horses, cats and flowers, so these scenes were etched on the boulder and now when I look at it I remember him and his love of animals and nature.

6. INCLUDE A MEMORY BOOK IN YOUR FUNERAL SERVICE.

Several of my friends left an open book at the chapel so family and friends could share their memories of the loved one. This ritual helped them as they read the many stories of their loved one.

7. IMMORTALIZE YOUR LOVED ONE WITH A SPECIAL FUND.

There are different organizations in every area that are worthy and needy. I donated to the Victorian Order of Nurses Fund in memory of my loved ones. The organization created a plaque etched with names of the deceased and now I can go to the local park and sit by a waterfall surrounded by greenery and view the names on the wall. Many funeral homes and hospitals also have a memorial wall for families that they cared for.

RESOURCES

1. *Multicultural Funeral Practices: A Guide To Funeral Customs in Canada* by Ontario Funeral Service Association, 1998
Many customs and religious beliefs are explained in this guidebook.

2. *Building Memories: Planning a Meaningful Funeral* by Doug Manning (In-Sight Books Inc., 1998)
A guide to planning a meaningful funeral, information on the types of ceremonies, the steps in planning a funeral, and how to personalize the service. I have attended several conferences held by Doug Manning. He is a compassionate man who writes from his experience as a clergy, a counsellor and a bereaved brother.

3. *Planning a Meaningful Cremation Burial* by Doug Manning (In-Sight Books, Inc., 2002)
A guide for families planning to cremate a loved one, including sections on family discussion, and planning the service. Several of my clients read this as they prepared for their final journey on earth.

4. *Creating Meaningful Funeral Ceremonies: A Guide For Caregivers* by Alan D. Wolfelt, PhD (Companion Press, 1994)
This guide assists caregivers in creating special ceremonies for loved ones and helps them during the grieving process.

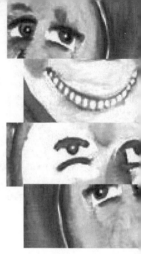

CHAPTER 3

BUILDING A
SUPPORTIVE NETWORK

Whether our loss was sudden or expected, we all grieve. Journeying through the grieving process is made easier – both physically and emotionally – when you benefit from the love of others. Family, friends and neighbours can all become an integral part of a supportive network that will buoy you up when you feel your loss pulling you down. This chapter will outline myriad ways in which support can mitigate grief and how best to reach out.

The importance of having nurturing people in your life as you journey through grief is crucial to healing. I want to share with you how I reached out to my family, friends and community during my roller-coaster ride through grief. (Even though it's been six years since my husband, Rhod, died, I still need the support of friends occasionally.) No, support does not make the grief go away – it will stay with you, become part of you – but it will help you return to a healthy, happy life.

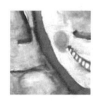

PHYSICAL NEEDS

Grief can be debilitating, so you'll need help with the following:

~ paperwork associated with the death (application
   for pensions, insurance);

~ meal preparation;

~ housekeeping;

~ grocery shopping;

~ answering the telephone and returning calls;

~ errands;

~ child care;

~ pet care;

~ transportation to medical appointments;

~ lawn care/snow removal.

EMOTIONAL NEEDS

~ non-judgmental ears (listen, even if I say the
   same things over and over);

~ endless time (my grieving process is my own
   and will not adhere to a timetable);

~ positive perspective (help me see that there
   are still people in my life who love me).

COMMUNITY AND FRIENDS TO LEAN ON

I always knew that I had people around me who loved me, but I had no idea how vital that love could be. When my son Steven and granddaughter Tate died, I depended on my husband, Rhod, for support; when he died I was lost – until I turned to my loving friends and family.

I grew up in a small town in Newfoundland. Everyone knew me, my seven siblings and the grandparents, aunts, uncles and cousins who all lived in the community, and all of us attended the town's one church and one school. Pulling together in times of crisis was a part of the town's culture. When I went through my own crises, turning to my community wasn't just natural, it was reflexive.

But when my loved ones died, there were 15 years and thousands of miles separating me from that immensely comforting childhood support structure. I might as well have been inhabiting a distant planet. At least, that's how I felt – at first. Over time, however, I learned a couple of valuable lessons:

Valuable Lesson Number One: Reaching out is a two-way street. My old friends couldn't be with me, so I went to them, staving off the isolation that makes the grieving process longer and harder. And the more I opened myself up to love, the more love they gave. It came in the form of cards and letters, of course, but on every trip home (and I made a point of making many) there were surprise visits and invitations to dinner. Every hug told me I was cared about.

Stop shutting yourself off from the outside world.

Losing your loved one is very difficult. I experienced many, many dark days and in these days I did not want to see anyone or take part in any activity. But I knew that I had to push myself and think positively despite the pain and turmoil.

Valuable Lesson Number Two: Create community wherever you find yourself. When my family and I moved from the Maritimes to Ontario, the tight network of friends and family became less readily available. That was hard. But I needed to let go of one community so that I could make room for another. While I missed my family and friends, I knew I needed supportive people in my day-to-day life. So I joined a new church community, joined the Girl Guides and became a leader, volunteered and became active in my work and continuing education. The investment I made in my new community served me well in my times of need.

Stop being the expert.

Learn to separate your professional role and your personal roles. I worked in palliative and bereavement care and this was one of my stumbling blocks in mourning for Steven and Tate. When Rhod died, I realized I had to stop giving advice and accept support. I didn't want to be caregiver...I wanted to be a caretaker.

NANCY AND ME

NANCY AND I HAD BEEN FRIENDS FOR 18 YEARS. WE
met at my workplace in 1982 when she started to work
there. I was fortunate enough to orient her in her job as a
team clerk. She was going through a difficult time – her
husband had been admitted to chronic care in the local
hospital and Nancy needed to make changes in her life, so
she decided to return to the workforce after being home
raising a family for 20 years.

Like most friends, we've been through life's ups and downs
together. I was with Nancy when her own husband died of
multiple sclerosis. Though Nancy was suffering, she and I
both learned something valuable. Loneliness is a void that
must be filled. Empty days and nights have to be booked
up with intimate connections, fun and learning. That was

something I helped Nancy with when she suffered her own loss. When I suffered mine, she was right there.

Develop a 'new' normal.

Your life will not be the same again. Your life changed when your loved one died. When Steven died, I had two children instead of three. When Tate died I had one grandchild instead of two. When Rhod died, half of my family was gone. When a piece of intact china is dropped on the floor, it will shatter into many pieces. When you try to put these pieces back together, it is impossible to shape it the way it was originally. It is forever changed. You are forever changed by your losses.

She listened to me for as long as I needed to talk through my pain and she never judged – two critical components of a good grief buddy. She encouraged me to embrace the beautiful memories of my son Steven when he died; and she reminded me that I was in a wonderful profession, one where I could help others who are in worse situations, instead of dwelling on my pain. Then, when the talking was done, she would force me to do something, anything, whether it was a walk, a skate or a movie. We even went to New York City for a fun-filled weekend. Nancy was a very positive woman who had a very positive effect on me. She helped me learn to laugh and, importantly, not to feel guilty about it. She was always a phone call away. Knowing that got me through many hard moments.

We both decided that it was okay to have a 'pity party,' but we refused to allow ourselves to spend too much time feeling sorry for ourselves. Instead, Nancy invited close friends of ours for a sleepover. We ordered pizza from our favourite place, Firenze's, watched chick flicks, drank wine, ate decadent foods and shared a lot of laughs. I remember laughing hysterically at one story Nancy told, about how when she was almost blown off a dock in Brockville, Ontario, while she was wearing a beautiful gown and high heels. The point of it all was to be surrounded by friends and have a great time.

And there were moments Nancy helped me celebrate Steven's life. On the first anniversary after Steven's death, Nancy and another friend, Carol, brought me a rose of Sharon bush to plant in the backyard in memory of Steven.

Other friends honoured his life too. One month after his death, on what would have been his birthday, Steven's friends came by the house to plant a maple tree in our backyard. They stayed for dinner and we all went to the cemetery together.

Recognize that you may be on grief overload.

You may have had several deaths in your family in a short time. My son, granddaughter and husband all died within seven years and within that time frame I had many special friends and volunteers from work die, too. I was losing many people in my life and this created many stressors. Recognizing the overload made it easier to accept support.

GRIEF AND DREAM JOURNALING

You may have nightmares for a few weeks or months after the death of a loved one. Keep a journal on your bedside table and record your dreams when you wake up. I found dream journaling to be a vital lifeline.

Rhod and I had spent a dreamy week in Mexico. Less than 24 hours after returning, he was in a London, Ontario, trauma unit fighting for his life. He spent 30 days in that unit before dying, and I was plagued by nightmares of those four weeks. Recording, in as much detail as possible, the events of each dream really helped me work through my pain.

I consider myself a strong person with an equally strong will to live. Still, I didn't know how to translate that will into an action plan. Journaling helped me take feelings from the inside to the outside, where I could examine them more rationally.

Similarly, writing about your grief may help you release pent-up pain. Maybe you find yourself without sufficient support, maybe you're just an exceedingly private person – whatever your situation, take the time to write about what you're experiencing. It worked for me. If this process doesn't work for you, seek counselling.

BECKY AND ME

BECKY WAS SAFE TO BE WITH BECAUSE SHE KNEW ME
and my family very well. We have been friends for 28
years and she is the next best thing to a sister. She missed
Rhod too. She let me talk about Rhod many times and we
shared many funny stories. She let me be me and did not
judge my feelings, even when I went from laughing one
minute to anger the next.

For the first six months after Rhod's death she drove me
to medical appointments, the grocery store, and countless
other destinations. She became my constant grief companion,
making it easier for me to give in to my feelings. She also
walked with me three to four times a week, getting me out
of the house and, briefly, out of my grief.

At the first sight of spring, Rhod and I regularly visited
local nurseries to shop for flowers and shrubs. We usually

spent hours and lots of money buying plants. Three months after Rhod died, I made the trip to my local nursery with Becky. I remember looking at all the colourful rose bushes – the red, yellow, white, orange ones – the ones Rhod especially loved. I remember how he loved planting them in our backyard. I reached to touch a yellow rose and its thorn pricked me. My finger hurt and it bled, and I remember telling Becky that's how my heart felt. She placed her arm around me and reminded me, "You'll heal in time." I didn't believe her then, but I knew she was right.

Don't be afraid to reach out to others.

Call a friend when you are feeling lost and lonely. Don't wait for them to call you. Tell your family what you are feeling now. Be honest and open. In the past you may have had problems with some family members and drifted apart. Don't wait for them to resolve the problem. Pick up the phone and call them or write them a note. Reconnect with friends that you have not talked to in a long time and renew the friendship.

Coping With Disappointing Friends

I REMEMBER VISITING A GROCERY STORE SEVERAL MONTHS after Rhod died and I ran into a friend who did not attend his funeral. She saw me, looked down and ran the other way. She could not deal with me. I met her again at a social function a year later and did not give her a chance to run away. I marched right up to her and said bluntly, "You find it difficult to talk to me, don't you?" She nodded, silently. Then she went on to explain that because I had suffered three major losses in a short time she was overwhelmed. She had no idea how to support that level of loss and was paralyzed by her own sense of inadequacy.

Loss can be an opportunity for growth if we choose that path.

When the fog cleared in my head, mind and soul, I searched inward and recognized that I am responsible for my own happiness. My happiness had been wrapped up in Rhod and now he was gone.

In the days and months following a loss, there will be many who step forward and many more who step away. What's amazing to me is not the support I received from some, but rather the lack of it from others. Friends who didn't show up at the funeral, or in the days and months after; acquaintances who attempted to hurry along recovery with tactless comments – "You're young; you'll get married again." Or, "You'll feel better in a few months."

RETAIL THERAPY

A very wise woman – Rhod's 88-year-old Aunt Prissie – once advised me to take on the bad days with a lot of forgiveness and a little shopping. She was right! Getting out of the house on a shopping expedition serves two purposes: it gets you out of your grief, at least temporarily, and adds some excitement to life as you hunt for something sinfully new. But the most important part of her message is to accept bad days for what they are – normal, natural and no one's fault, least of all your own.

It's important that you don't allow those disappointments to feed your grief. People will say all the wrong things, but you'll need to remember that they are not the best part of your support network. I learned to avoid the people who I knew would attempt to minimize my grief, but I forgave them because their life experiences were different from mine. Eventually, I got to a point in my grief journey when I didn't feel like people who weren't supportive were sucking the energy out of me.

Several of our long-time friends did not attend Rhod's funeral. One of them told me later that he could not cope; seeing someone so young and so close to his own age die was too much for him to deal with. Another friend had lost her own husband only a few months earlier and just couldn't revisit that pain so soon. I learned to forgive them for their own difficulties dealing with my grief. They were human and did the best they could at a difficult time.

We, the bereaved, may have to teach others about loss. Most people truly want to be there to support us, but don't know how. By sharing my own story, and the many stories of support, maybe they'll know how to help others go down the grief road. I have realized through my losses that I have unique experiences that make me who I am; my family and friends have their own unique experiences along their own life journeys. I keep calling myself a "Tragic Optimist," meaning that despite the tragedies in my life I remain positive.

SUPPORT LOSSES

Even if your loved one died after a long illness, following much discussion and planning, grief is inevitable – and, in fact, is in many ways unique. While friends and family may expect your grief to be brief, many left behind suffer not only a normal grieving process, but also experience the added loss of a caregiving role they had become accustomed to while caring for a loved one.

❧ From My Journal ❧

March 19, 1999 – I can't seem to get the energy to write, but I must force myself to put these feelings on paper. I go over things in my mind and I feel as if I'm going crazy. I feel so empty. I still can't believe this is happening to me. I feel so closed in, suffocated – especially when I'm with someone who is talking nonstop. I must tell them what I need. I must reach out to people who will support me. I can't support them anymore – I have nothing to give.

March 23, 1999 – I am thinking of my friend Nancy. I hear her voice and I feel her around me. She is telling me that I must eat and I must rest. I remember the conversations that we had when her husband died. My head is so muddled but I think her spirit is reaching out to me and supporting me at this moment.

March 25, 1999 – Dentist appointment. The doctor did not acknowledge Rhod's death. He has been our family dentist for over a decade. Very strange. His office called me two days after Rhod's death to book an appointment for Rhod. I was very upset then and am more upset now. I expected a kind word and a little support. I feel angry now.

May 31, 1999 – I returned to work. I knew many people and they reached out to support me with kind words and hugs. I made it through, but now feel exhausted. This is difficult. I have to rest.

December 4, 1999 – Went to a Christmas party with Carol. I was a little anxious about going and I almost cancelled. It was difficult. People kept asking how I was doing and telling me how strong I was and that they were so happy to see me. It was good to have the support, but I found it very draining.

Strategies: Finding Support

Here are some ways to give yourself a boost of support.

1. **SURROUND YOURSELF WITH GOOD LISTENERS.**

   Seek out at least two or three friends who are good listeners. You need to tell your story over and over until you believe it and accept it.

2. **JOIN A BEREAVEMENT SUPPORT GROUP.**

   Being with people who have suffered similar losses will help you feel not so alone in your grief. I had several friends who were widows and we socialized on a regular basis. Some of your friends may know someone with a similar loss; ask them to introduce you.

3. **LEARN A NEW LANGUAGE.**

   What better way to meet new people and learn Spanish, German or French at the same time?

4. **JOIN A STAMP CLUB, BOOK CLUB, TOASTMASTERS.**

   Surround yourself with your friends but also strive to meet new people. I joined an investment club for women one year after Rhod died and enjoyed the experience while learning about the stock market.

5. **HOST A DINNER PARTY.**

   Invite your friends over for dinner. If it is too much to do all the cooking yourself, suggest a potluck.

6. **HAVE A FRIEND MOVE IN FOR THE FIRST WEEK.**

My pal Dorothy (from Newfoundland) came to stay with me, making herself available 24-7. That really helped me get over the hurdle of those first few painful days and long, long nights.

7. **CONNECT REGULARLY BY TELEPHONE.**

My mother telephoned me almost daily for a year after my husband died, helping me feel connected and loved.

8. **LEAN ON NEIGHBOURS.**

There will be many small, but tiresome, household chores that threaten to overwhelm. Call in reinforcements. My neighbours Pat and Jack cut my grass, shovelled my driveway and looked after my cats, freeing me to rejoin life at my own pace.

9. **MAKE REGULAR DATES WITH FRIENDS.**

I bought season's tickets to the symphony and went monthly with one friend; with another I went for a weekly movie or dinner. I didn't always want to go, but I made myself get out, and over time those regular outings reconnected me to my world and the people in it.

10. **GET ON A PLANE.**

Get away from over-familiar surroundings and make new friends in faraway places. My friend Carol, who is originally from Ireland, invited me to go with her to Ireland 18 months after Rhod died. I spent three weeks with her family and was completely renewed.

RESOURCES

1. *Man's Search For Meaning* by Viktor Frankl (Washington Square Press Publication of Pocket Books, 1959)
I read this book at least 10 times. I was inspired by reading Viktor Frankl's story of survival in a concentration camp. If he could survive, I could too. Sometimes I would only read a line or a page. His words brought me hope and support.

2. *Don't Sweat The Small Stuff With Your Family; Don't Sweat The Small Stuff At Work*, both by Richard Carlson, PhD (Hyperion, 1998)
I read these books a year after Rhod died. Richard Carlson's books are inspirational and helped me to stay positive for longer periods of time.

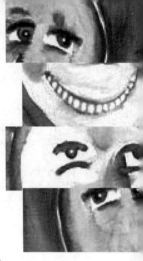

CHAPTER 4

GUILT AND THE
WHAT IFS

You'll experience a flood of emotions when a loved one dies. One of them is guilt, and it's a normal reaction to grief – whether a loved one's death was sudden, a suicide, or anticipated – for deeds left undone or words unspoken. We may even feel guilty for being alive or for profiting in some way because of a loved one's death. And our guilt may be compounded by the reaction of others, our inability to express our anger or anxiety and remorse over a certain action that resulted in the person's death. But guilt can't be left unchecked. By not resolving our guilt, we can delay our grief or put it on hold for years, which can subsequently harm us further physically and emotionally.

It's important to acknowledge and respect our feelings even though they may not be well founded. This chapter will focus on the importance of resolving our guilt, remorse and regret. By giving these feelings a voice, you lessen their control over you during your grief journey.

MY STORY

HOW GUILT HURT ME

The circumstances surrounding the death of my son Steven (1992), granddaughter Tate (1994), and husband, Rhod (1999), were all different; so were my relationships with each one of them, and it affected my feelings of guilt and the grief journey that followed.

When Steven died of suicide, I naturally felt an enormous amount of regret and guilt. He was my child, and the fact that he died before me and that he took his life only compounded my guilt. I kept reviewing in my mind how I could have changed the situation. "If only I had insisted he get long-term counselling after his first attempt three years before he died."; "Why did I not see that he was depressed?"; "Maybe if I wasn't so busy with my own life, I could have helped him." I felt the most guilt for what I didn't do on the day he died – I didn't follow my own intuition. Somehow, I had a strong sense that something 'bad' was going to happen that day. But, I shrugged off my inner voice and labelled it as paranoia. Later that night, we received a dreadful phone call confirming my worst fear.

Before I could even mourn Steven's death, I had to deal with the trauma of this entire experience. In a sudden death, homicide, suicide or other violent death, the mind has a difficult time absorbing and acknowledging the circumstances of a death. I was only able to deal with it by repeatedly telling my story to my counsellor, Sister St. John from Sarnia, even though I didn't resolve my guilt until Rhod died seven years later.

UNLOCKING GUILT

IT WAS ONLY WHEN I MOURNED OPENLY, THAT IS, SHARED my feelings publicly while taking counselling courses years later that I could face the guilt I felt after Steven's death head-on. Before my breakthrough moment, I was working with people who were dying and bereaved and I was constantly told that I was strong. So, I continually pushed down my feelings of guilt when they surfaced.

In the counselling class, we were forced to deal with our own losses before we could genuinely help others deal with their losses. I remember being in a training session

Recognize that guilt is a natural feeling when we have a loss.

It's important that we explore our feelings of guilt, work on resolving them and then move forward. Even after you've overcome the guilt, it's normal to feel twinges of guilt resurface. I remember feeling guilty when I travelled to Ireland after Rhod died because we had planned on going to Europe the year of his death.

with 18 bereavement caregivers who each told their own story about losing a loved one, some recounted similar experiences to mine. I felt safe in this group, and when we broke out into smaller groups, I was finally able to share my guilt and pain for the first time since Steven died. I felt vulnerable when I first shared my thoughts, but I also felt a sense of relief because I realized I was not the only person with these feelings. Now I could finally share them without being judged as a failure.

Channel your energy into worthwhile causes.

Focusing on others will help you take your mind off yourself for a while. Maybe start a suicide survivor support group or a widow/widower support group, depending on your loss. Sharing your guilt with others will help them feel like they're not alone.

Over time, I realized that Steven was ultimately responsible for his own actions. I had tried to offer him support after his marriage broke down, one of the reasons why he hit rock bottom just before his death. By expressing my feelings of guilt, I was able to dwell on the special times I had shared with Steven. In turn, my self-esteem grew and I could admit that I am not perfect, but rather human.

Two years later, when my granddaughter Tate died shortly after her birth, I felt guilty because my daughter, Lexine, wouldn't experience the same joy I had, seeing my three children grow up. I was angry at the medical system because I thought my daughter's family physician should have been monitoring her more closely. Having gone through childbirth, I also felt a sense of regret that I hadn't encouraged Lexine, who was two weeks overdue with Tate at 10 pounds at birth, to consider being induced earlier. I kept thinking, "Would Tate have lived?" I supported Lexine as best I could and tried not to dwell on what could have been.

Two years later, my good friend Nancy died. Again, guilt overwhelmed me because she had supported me throughout my losses, but I wasn't able to be with her at the end of her life. Her family had requested family-only visits during the last month of her life in the hospital. I was angry that I was not allowed to see her. I also felt guilty later that I had let her down because I knew that she would have wanted me at her bedside.

Just when I thought I was making progress in my grief journey, even though I hadn't properly addressed my guilt issues, Rhod died. I knew that in order for me to heal, I had to deal with every other unresolved emotion I had experienced during my other losses. On top of that, Rhod's death brought other feelings of guilt,

Practice forgiveness.

It's hard enough forgiving others, but it can be even harder to forgive ourselves. We must give ourselves permission to do so. When my son Steven died, I wrote him a letter to forgive him and myself.

mainly because I felt a sense of relief that he was no longer suffering from all the invasive hospital procedures he had endured over the last month of his life. I also felt guilty for not being able to grant Rhod his wish of forgoing life support.

To deal with my feelings of guilt, I wrote my feelings down in a personal journey. By putting them down on paper, I would be forced to deal with my guilt without feeling judged by others. I think that's when I made up my mind to write this book to help others.

Realize that you are human.

We're all human and imperfect, but family and societal pressures can cause us much misery. However, we can change that – we create most of the stress in our lives and give people permission to hurt us. Don't look at the mistakes as mistakes, but rather as life experiences.

Beating Yourself Up

WHEN A LOVED ONE DIES, WE ARE APT TO REMEMBER first and foremost the unresolved issues in the relationship. We tend to remember the struggles before we can think of the good times and the joy the relationship brought. As a result, we deal with the guilt of not having made more out of our relationship before a loved one died.

It's especially the case with suicide survivor guilt, which was a monumental struggle for me. One well-meaning person said to me, "It must be awful that Steven died, but to commit suicide, you must feel very guilty?" Another woman said, "Didn't you see the signs?" After hearing these remarks, I

Learn to grow through your losses.

Use your loss to grow as a person – maybe you could explore a career change, take a risk with a home business, or become a mentor. As a grief survivor, you now have the qualifications to reach for that dream.

couldn't help thinking that I may not have been the best mother. Suicide survivors will definitely feel more guilt, but it doesn't mean that the guilt can't be resolved. It's human nature to have feelings of guilt no matter what the circumstances of death. How you deal with guilt will depend on how your loved one died, on your relationship with the person, your coping abilities, your loss experience and your support network. While the circumstances around my loved ones' deaths were traumatic for the most part, I was fortunate enough to be able to draw support from my friends, remaining family and the people I worked with, including the volunteers and staff at the Victorian Order of Nurses Volunteer Services and my peers at Community Care Access Centre.

Spend time at the cemetery.

Visiting the cemetery was a haven for me. I often planted flowers on my son's and husband's plots as I spoke to them. It gave me hope and peace of mind. I was also surrounded by nature – I listened to the birds sing and watched the flowers grow.

I felt rejection when Steven died because I thought he did not love us enough to stay around and he was telling us that we could not help him. But, over time and with a lot of support, I was able to understand his despair and his feelings of inadequacy and powerlessness. I was able to understand his unresolved grief by doing a review of Steven's life. When Steven was young, he didn't adjust well when we moved across the country, especially because his best friend died weeks before the move. Later in life, he found it difficult dealing with the breakup of his marriage and the loss of his daughter, who went to live with her mother.

Unresolved Guilt

WHEN WE DON'T DEAL WITH GUILT, IT WILL AFFECT US both emotionally and physically. Emotionally, guilt can destroy your self-esteem and weigh heavily on your mind and soul, sometimes turning you into a bitter, unhappy person. Guilt can also prolong grief or put it on hold for years. Physically, guilt can cause feelings of anxiety, anger, remorse and denial. For example, calling a suicide an accident will only prolong your grief and mourning because you'd be living with a lie until you faced the truth, that is, a loved one intended to take his or her life. At its worst, unresolved guilt could lead to depression. Until you find a safe place to share those feelings, you can't move forward in your healing journey. We can reconcile guilt by telling our story over and over again until we are able to integrate it into our lives.

Guilt in Degrees

While guilt is a natural reaction to death, it can vary – for some, guilt can be monumental and for others, it is minuscule, depending on the relationship with the deceased. The important thing is to recognize these feelings and work to resolve them. Here are some scenarios in which people feel some degree of guilt following the death of a loved one:

1. My mother cared for my grandmother (she died in 2002 at the age of 99) in her home for 13 years. In the last eight months before she died, my grandmother was placed in a long-term care facility. My mom was the total caregiver without respite, but she still had guilty feelings for admitting her mom to a facility. While she didn't have a choice, it still didn't lessen her feelings of guilt.

2. My friend Janet lost her teenage daughter, Lori, to Septic Shock Syndrome. Lori experienced flu-like symptoms on a Sunday, became progressively worse and died several days later when admitted to hospital. Despite the physician's assurance that the family acted appropriately, Janet was still

overwhelmed with guilt because she went out of town on that Sunday. Janet suppressed her guilt so much that she was unable to cope with life. Counselling later helped her put a voice to her feelings and she created an annual scholarship fund in the name of her daughter.

3. Another friend, whose husband died after a long illness, felt deep resentment during his illness because he became controlling and demanding of her time and energy, and then she felt guilty over her feelings of resentment when he died.

4. The husband of one of my clients died two months after contracting an occupational disease. She struggled with the guilt of inheriting a large sum of money from the Workplace Safety & Insurance Board. Her husband was on the brink of retiring and was making plans for their future. Now her goals and dreams were all gone and she wanted her husband back, not the money. She later accepted his loss and knew that he was at peace knowing she was well cared for financially.

From My Journal

May 12, 1999 – This is a horrible time for me right now. I am mourning Rhod, but I feel guilty that I am not thinking of Steven as much. And then I feel I should think about Tate. My head is spinning. Where do I go from here? I must think and sort this out. I feel overwhelmed. I don't have control of my life anymore.

November 26, 1999 – Steven is very deep in my thoughts today. The pain hit me like a ton of bricks on my chest and I can barely breathe. I feel as if I am having a heart attack.

I'm feeling regret and I'm angry that he is not here to see Lyndsay grow up. So many feelings all at once to deal with.

I think about when we moved to Ontario and he didn't want to move and always yearned to go back east. Would he be living today if we had not made the move? I think about when his best friend, Paul, died of leukemia and then we moved to Ontario a few weeks later. I reflect on Steven's many losses, most of them unresolved, and ask myself why I didn't see this back then. Now it is so easy to see, but I can't do anything about it.

August 13, 2002 – Feeling good today. Much joy in my life. It has been such a roller-coaster ride to get to this point in my journey. I have worked through my guilt, anguish, regrets and what ifs, but I do not know if these feelings will surface again when I'm least expecting them to. I know that this is a normal part of my journey and I will learn to embrace my feelings and let them go. I feel that I am in control of my world again and don't feel the chaos. I'm healing but I realize I still have to journey further. I pray that I can heal somewhat before the next big loss occurs.

Strategies: Turning Off The Voice

We can tame the guilt voice so it doesn't take over our lives by being honest with ourselves, and sharing the feelings of guilt with others. Here are some additional strategies to help turn off the inner voice.

1. SHINE YOUR BEACON.

When I reached a certain point in resolving guilt and remorse I made a pact with myself – take my pain and turn it around to help others. I went on an inward journey to explore my gifts and then offered them to others. So, I took some continuing education courses and began my counselling practice.

2. LIVE A HASSLE-FREE LIFE.

My losses created a well within me that is full of gratitude. I don't tolerate the 'bull' anymore and I know I don't have to answer to anyone. I can verbally express my views and don't make any apologies for doing so.

3. REACH OUT TO GOD FOR MEANING.

For me, prayer was beneficial in helping me resolve my guilt. I often asked for guidance and strength to bear the pain of my losses. My God is a loving and compassionate

God and I feel his presence and grace when I feel a sense of guilt within me.

4. **BEFRIEND YOUR GRIEF.**

Grief can drag you down if you let it. You must befriend it and understand that feelings of guilt, remorse and anger are normal. Any additional loss will bring with it new feelings, but also a resurgence of unresolved feelings and emotions. Be aware that you may need to do more grief work with the previous loss, too.

5. **KEEP A POSITIVE SPIN ON LIFE.**

Love yourself despite your broken spirit and heart. You need to explore and work through your emotions associated with our loss. Suppressing your feelings of guilt will only lower your confidence and self-esteem. Until I was able to deal with these emotions, I felt empty and sad. Thinking positive and verbalizing what I was feeling helped me to release these negative (normal) feelings.

RESOURCES

1. *Slow Time 101 Poems To Take You There* by Niall MacMonagle (Marino Books, 2000).
My friend Cathy from Ireland gave me this beautiful book of poetry. It provides commentary on the personal experiences that shape our lives, whether they be death, love, laughter, sorrow or old age. I highly recommend it when you feel a twinge of guilt or remorse.

2. *Bridges: A Journal of Transition* by Susan Duxter (New Image Strategies, 1991).
I went to this motivational seminar two years after my son died. This speaker/author was very energetic as she recounted her personal stories of pain, loss and coping. This book will motivate you and give you a sense of hope.

3. *It isn't Always Easy But Know That I Care*, edited by Susan Polis Schutz (Blue Mountain Press, 1982).
A collection of poems about the struggles and pain in our lives and how support can help us. My friend Nancy gave me this book when Steven died.

4. *Writing your Way Through Personal Crisis, Pain And Possibility* by Gabriele Lussor Rico (Jeremy P. Tarcher Inc., 1991).
I bought this book a couple of months after Rhod died. It talks about how to transform your emotional pain and personal tragedy into new possibilities for personal growth using your own words on a page. It also offers many tools and techniques to help you express your pain.

CHAPTER 5

MAKING DECISIONS
FOR THE FUTURE

Making changes, good or bad ones, throughout life is never easy. When you lose a loved one, especially a spouse, dealing with changes becomes even more trying. Suddenly, you face the daunting task of making decisions about funeral arrangements, financial planning, living arrangements and employment options. Only now, you're making decisions at a time when you're feeling confused, abandoned and fearful of many things, including your security.

Here, in this chapter, I've outlined some of the decisions you'll be forced to make and the emotions behind them.

MY STORY

DECISIONS ABOUT LIFE, DEATH, FINANCES AND WORK

When my husband, Rhod, died my view of the world changed. I lost my self-identity, my security and my confidence. I was a "widow," and I hated the term. I remember getting angry when I had to complete Canada Pension forms and check off the box that said widow under marital status. And there was the time when I went on an Alaskan cruise in 1999 – I told people who asked if I was married that "my husband died and I'm single again" rather than use the W-word.

I had never lived alone before Rhod's death, so I never had to worry about small things like shovelling my driveway, mowing the lawn or servicing my car.

Small, everyday decisions now became major decisions. And several major decisions were now my responsibility too, such as planning for my financial future. I had to take care of Rhod's pension, our retirement funds, our stock investments, a car purchase and the everyday house bills that Rhod and I once shared together.

I had to accept that life would be different and that I could not deal with all the changes and the decision-making that came with them. To help me, I leaned on family and friends for advice and support. My

Don't let people take advantage of you.

You're vulnerable at this stage, so before you make a major decision take extra time and get advice if you need it. Get any information or quotes in writing. For example, I ordered Rhod's memorial and paid for it in full ($3,476) before I received it. When it arrived, it was not what I had ordered and the company refused to reimburse me or re-order it even though I had all my documentation. I finally received my money, but only after going through court mediation.

friend and neighbour Jack shovelled my driveway the first winter after Rhod's death and I hired a service the second winter. I remember being determined to cut the grass on my own the first summer and I called my daughter, Lexine, for a lesson on how to use the lawn mower. A couple of years later, I bulked up for more physical tasks by joining a local gym and starting a light weights training program. My routines changed too. I went to my daughter's after church on Sunday for the first year and dropped in for dinner a couple times a week. I invited my friends over or went on outings with them – anything not to spend time home alone. In general, it took me about 18 months to fully adjust to living alone and the responsibilities that came with it.

MEDICAL DECISIONS

ON THE 30TH DAY OF RHOD'S HOSPITALIZATION I MADE the decision to cease medical intervention. I knew that Rhod died within 24 hours after his hospitalization but he was kept alive because he was in a teaching hospital and he didn't designate a power of attorney for his personal care.

I knew he wouldn't welcome all of the invasive procedures over the month he was kept alive, but my hands were tied. Then, finally, on February 6th, 1999, I insisted the medical staff cease medical interventions. Even though one of the resident physicians later told me that I had made the right decision, I had been struggling with it and

Don't forget to laugh often.

Rhod was big on bringing me flowers, and after he died I made a decision to carry on the tradition. When friends stopped by and saw a beautiful bouquet of flowers, they'd usually say jokingly, "You must have an admirer." My response would be, "Yes, Rhod is still sending me flowers. Isn't he wonderful!?"

preparing my family for a couple of weeks. I was familiar with death but it was different this time – I was emotionally involved.

We had to then make the tough decision of saying yes to an autopsy. My children and I made the decision together, as we did to cease medical intervention. We didn't want Rhod to undergo anymore invasive procedures even after death, but we wanted to know the exact cause of death. We learned Rhod had pancreatitis; knowing this was helpful to my family in finding closure and putting a name to the disease that caused his death.

Get a grip on your financial situation.

It's never too late to be proactive in your finances. I joined an investment club for women a year after Rhod died to become more familiar with the terminology of the stock market while learning about different companies. It was also an opportunity to get out and have fun with 22 other women. I also attended several financial seminars for the first three years to continue to build my confidence.

FUNERAL ARRANGEMENTS

I WAS OVERWHELMED WITH GRIEF AND SHOCK EVEN though Rhod had been hospitalized for weeks. I had to now think about planning a funeral. I wanted to honour Rhod's wonderful life and welcome the support of friends and family, but it took an enormous amount of energy from within to pull it off. With my family's support, I designated various members a task and hired the same funeral director who had assisted with my son Steven's and granddaughter Tate's funerals. I wanted the event to not only be a celebration of Rhod's life but also an opportunity to help facilitate the grief of my loved ones.

You can become a valuable resource to others.

By helping others make decisions during their grief journey you can help yourself. Whether you're a lawyer, accountant, banker, counsellor or administrator, sharing your skills will help you gain strength, confidence and meaning in your life.

I decided to have Rhod's body buried instead of cremated because this was a part of my cultural history. I arranged to have his resting place close to Steven's and Tate's, who were also buried in the same cemetery. It helped me emotionally and spiritually to know that Rhod's body would still be with us for some time.

I arranged for two funeral visitations. That meant we wouldn't be burying Rhod until three days later, but I wanted to give family and friends the opportunity to support us and say their goodbyes. We had a United Church service (our church community) and were involved with selecting the

Find growth in your decision-making.

I may have made some decisions that caused me some pain, but I learned from these decisions. For example, if you've made a wrong financial decision, use the opportunity to become proactive and learn about your finances. My decision to take early retirement in 2000 has given me many rewards emotionally and spiritually.

scripture readings, hymns and other aspects of the service. Our daughter, Lexine, and her cousin Kelly did the eulogy along with several of Rhod's co-workers, who shared memories of him.

There were other small, personal touches as part of the service. For example, everyone in the family helped to make a photo collage of Rhod's life. It served two purposes – it brought us some tears and laughter as we recounted our memories of life with Rhod and it helped us to grieve and support one another. The collage was later displayed at the funeral home and the church hall, where a reception followed the burial.

Financial Issues

FINANCIAL DECISIONS CAN CREATE HUGE STRESS DURING your grieving process. They can become so overwhelming at times that they can even put your grief on hold. I was terrified when I thought about my future – Will I have enough money to survive? Will I make the right decisions financially to benefit me in my future? How was I going to manage the cost of funeral expenses? Was I going to be able to stay in the family home?

To help me get these answers, I decided to hire Warren, a financial planner who was highly recommended. I learned from my friend Mary about the importance of bringing a professional on board early. When Mary lost her husband, she was financially stable but couldn't make an appointment with an advisor for several months after her husband's death. She felt guilty because she was now going to benefit from his death and delayed any financial decisions. In doing so, she had lost hundreds of dollars in interest because she neglected to invest benefits and monies sooner.

Before hiring Warren, I opted to take Rhod's pension from the company where he worked as a lump sum and invest it. At the time, I had no idea where to invest it, nor did I know what to do with the retirement funds we owned or the few stocks we held over the years when Rhod dabbled in the stock market.

I was glad to have Warren working for me two months after Rhod's death, especially to

Don't fret about the small stuff.

The bereaved have a tendency to worry, worry, worry. We worry about our security, our health, our finances, our social network, our family, and it causes our decision-making to be clouded. Instead, I channel the 'worry' energy into something positive and take things one day at a time, like when I decided to live alone.

deal with our stocks. I remember one occasion when Rhod bought several thousands of dollars of stock in pork futures that went down in several days. I was very upset with him even though he recouped it all in a few weeks when he bought a sugar stock. Naturally, I wasn't looking forward to making such stressful financial decisions without advice.

MARKED FOR STORAGE

There's no set time to pack a loved one's possessions. The best time is when it feels right for you. (It took me two years to let go of most of Rhod's possessions. It was a gradual process — sometimes one or two items at a time.) You may find it comforting to pack certain items in boxes but may not be able to part with them immediately, and that's okay. I moved all of Rhod's clothes to one closet a couple of months after his death, then slowly gave them away to loved ones and charitable organizations. It's okay to ask for help from family and friends too, but don't let them do it for you. This is an important part of your grief process, and it will help you bring closure on the death of a loved one.

Future Decisions

Living Arrangements

AFTER RHOD DIED I RECEIVED LOTS OF ADVICE ON WHERE to live. Some told me my home was too big for me and that I should consider selling my house and buying a smaller home. My son asked me to move to Windsor to be close to him and his family. My mom wanted me to move to Newfoundland. My Aunt Prissie wanted me to move to Toronto to live with her.

But I didn't want to move. I knew the importance of not making a major decision like moving residence for a minimum of one year. But, more importantly, my memories were all tied to my home. I didn't want to make more changes in my life at this time. Besides, I didn't have the energy to pack my belongings or get to know new neighbours. I just wanted to cocoon myself in my own home. I liked the city of Sarnia – it's where my daughter and her family lived, where I had a tight network of friends and great neighbours. Six years later, I'm still very happy to be here.

Work Changes

I returned to work on May 31, 1999, almost four months after Rhod's death. But I wasn't ready physically and emotionally. In fact, I was still under my physician's care months later.

I returned to work as the palliative care volunteer coordinator and dropped my additional responsibility as the acting program manager of volunteer services. I also reduced my work schedule from five to three days a week, in part because my

Legal Aid

In Canada, if you don't have the funds to hire a lawyer to settle a loved one's estate, contact your Legal Aid Department or your local member of parliament for assistance.

physician recommend I cut more of my workload and my employer offered little flexibility in my schedule. Still, it was difficult for me to work two consecutive days. Ultimately, I had to make a decision – my employer gave me the option to work either five or three days a week, nothing less. I took early retirement 18 months later and focused on studying and training to become a grief counsellor, a goal I had set shortly after my son Steven's death.

GRIEF ON HOLD

While dealing with financial issues, you could stop yourself from grieving a loved one or put your grief on hold temporarily. But it's never too late to grieve and mourn your loss. When the husband of one of my clients died, she did not grieve her loss until one year later. She was mired in the financial upheaval of her husband's business and she couldn't deal with the emotions surrounding his death until the estate was finally settled, one-and-a-half years later.

During my educational studies, I met many nurturing individuals who suffered many losses and now were giving back by helping others during their grieving process. It motivated me to stick to my career choice. In 2002, I set up my own private practice in grief counselling and continue to gain strength from helping others cope with their grief.

Friendships

After Rhod died, my relationships with many friends changed, especially with my couple friends. I was no longer a couple, so I didn't fit into their world. A few reached out by inviting me for dinner; many others stopped calling. I felt very lonely and, for some time, wondered if I had done something wrong to cause a rift between us. I realized that this wasn't my fault but simply their inability to adapt to a new relationship.

When I saw old friends in social settings I often thought about encouraging communication, but I didn't feel comfortable in pursuing their friendships if they hadn't contacted me. I made the decision not to pursue their friendships, but instead foster new ones. Besides, I had some great friends who continued to support me.

I found great comfort in many female friendships, which either remained the same or grew even stronger. Friends like Becky, Carol, Ingrid and Juanita were precious, and they always felt comfortable with me on my own since we were used to getting together when Rhod worked evening shifts. These friends also knew Rhod and listened to me talk over and over about my life with him, in addition to continuously bringing over home-cooked meals and sometimes accompanying me to the cemetery.

FUNERAL HOME SERVICES

You'll have some difficult and somewhat urgent decisions to make during the funeral arrangements for a loved one. To help you, here's a checklist of the type of services your funeral director may offer:

SPIRITUAL SERVICE: If you and your loved one did not have a church affiliation, your funeral director will recommend clergy to help you tailor the service to suit you and your family's needs. Remember the purpose of a memorial for your loved one is twofold: to help strengthen your faith and to begin your healing journey of grief.

RITUALS: Different rituals may be customary according to a loved one's culture. For example, you might choose cremation over a burial, or a memorial service instead of a funeral. Have your director review your choices in detail. You may even choose to hold a celebration of life or memorial ritual several months later. For other suggestions, ask family and friends about their rituals. (Also see Chapter 2, "The Value of Rituals.")

GRIEF SUPPORT: Many funeral homes provide group support for the bereaved at no charge. Ask for it if you need it.

PAPERWORK: You'll be supplied with a checklist of important paperwork you're responsible to file (see box "The Paper Trail" on the next page for more details).

The Paper Trail

At all times, it's important to keep accessible files on important government and financial records. Here's a listing of some of the documents you'll need to access to file appropriate documentation.

Death certificate: File the appropriate documentation, provided by the funeral home.

Marriage certificate: Original copy required when filing for any government pension.

Birth certificate: Original copy required when filing for any government pension.

Social insurance number (of the deceased): Required when filing for any government pension.

Original will (obtained from lawyer): Get in contact with the deceased's lawyer to arrange for a will presentation with family members. You'll also need a copy of the will when applying for any government pension, collecting life insurance or making any transactions.

Pension benefits (employer's and Canada Pension Plan): Your funeral director may provide the appropriate forms for CPP. Beneficiaries must apply for benefits under the Canada Pension Plan at the nearest office of the Department of National Health and Welfare. You'll be provided with a booklet called *Survivor's Benefits*.

Life insurance: If the deceased had life insurance, you'll need a copy of the will, death certificate and coroner's report before the company will process it.

Union/association benefits: If your loved one paid union or association dues, you may be entitled to funds, such as those that are paid out by the Workplace Safety & Insurance Board.

Assets/investments/loans: Make a list of joint property, assets and money owed and file the appropriate paperwork to transfer ownership to you where appropriate. (Banking institutions will require a copy of the will and death certificate if your spouse didn't have a joint account and/or to transfer RRSPs or RESPs.) Write down amounts, where they're stored/filed and contact info for credit cards, mortgage, RRSPs, bank accounts, investments, safety deposit box, real property and money owed. For example, Rhod and I jointly owned our assets, so our RRSPs were transferred to me when I provided the proper documentation (i.e., will, death certificate).

Medical files: Contact the deceased's family doctor if he/she is not aware of the patient's death and obtain medical files as a record of family medical history.

Dealing with Possessions

AS DIFFICULT AS IT IS TO SAY GOODBYE TO A LOVED ONE, it can be equally as difficult to let go of her belongings. Things such as clothes, jewellery, collections, etc., were once a part of a loved one's life, but once she has died they're the only tangible things that are left of her.

I was finally able to part with my son Steven's Grade 8 graduation suit a couple of summers ago, 10 years after his death. I still have his college books and some mementos.

I gave Rhod's truck to our son Gavin a few months after his father's death. Gavin also took many of his dad's tools, which he prized. I'm saving some jewellery for the grandchildren to give to them on significant occasions. Clothing was personal and I wanted certain people to have an item or two. Rhod's dad, for example, has one of his leather jackets. He may not wear it but I know he cherishes it. I gave the grandchildren T-shirts that they wore as pajamas for several months. I wore one of Rhod's shirts to bed for several weeks until I was ready to let it go. Our granddaughter Lyndsay loved his blanket, which reminded her of times when she snuggled up with Grandpa on the couch to watch *Star Trek* together.

SOURCE SUPPORT

With grieving comes clouded judgment. To help you make more focused, informed decisions, enlist the help of the following organizations and people.

FUNERAL DIRECTOR: Check the white or yellow pages, local funeral association or friends and family for referrals.

LAWYER: Consult with him/her regarding a will, whether it's important to get probate (which allows one or more people to deal with the estate), appropriate fees and other applicable legislation affecting an estate. Will and estate laws vary from province to province, or state to state. If you don't have a lawyer, check with family and friends or your regional law association. Since I was the executor and beneficiary of Rhod's estate, probate wasn't necessary.

BANKING INSTITUTION, INSURANCE COMPANY, ACCOUNTANT AND FINANCIAL PLANNER: When contacting these organizations, ask if you need to file any specific paperwork to update your records.

GRIEF AND BEREAVEMENT SUPPORT GROUP OR INDIVIDUAL COUNSELLING: Contact the Canadian Mental Health Association, a local hospice, a funeral home or community churches for recommendations.

FAMILY PHYSICIAN: Call for a complete health check and, if needed, ask for a referral for counselling services.

FAMILY AND FRIENDS: They can be a wealth of knowledge and experience to help you find appropriate professionals, from handymen assisting with household tasks to lawn maintenance companies to nannies or babysitters.

~ From My Journal ~

February 16, 1999 – Did not sleep last night. I have so much on my mind. I can't believe Rhod is gone. I have an appointment with our lawyer today. I don't want to go. I can't think. My brain is on hold. I'm scared of making the wrong decisions. My mind is wandering and I can even visualize that maybe I won't be able to make a decision. I have to take one step at a time and I know that Ray will give me good advice.

February 24, 1999 – I have so many decisions to make. Where do I turn? I have to call the bank. I have to call my lawyer again. I have to call Grant (funeral director). I have bills to pay. I have to make an appointment with my doctor. I must try to send a couple of thank you cards today, but I'm so tired.

March 1, 1999 – I'm so overwhelmed today. I must try to think about my roof. I have to get estimates for new shingles. I need the living room ceiling repaired but I guess that can be done after my roof is repaired. What if I get the wrong company? I really did not expect to have all of this responsibility, Rhod. It's too much. I can't handle this right now.

Strategies: Making the Right Decisions

Take your time and practice these strategies to make important decisions.

1. ACCESS RESOURCEFUL PEOPLE.

There are many people in your business and social circles who can be invaluable to you during this difficult time. Reach out to them to help you make necessary decisions and lighten your stress load. For example, my banking officer came to my home to discuss financial matters instead of meeting me at the bank.

2. WRITE A TO-DO LIST.

I kept a little book on daily tasks that I needed to complete and a separate book for my journal entries. And while the journal stayed on my kitchen table, the book followed me wherever I went to record phone calls, appointments, contact people and other details I wasn't sure I could remember.

3. EMPHASIZE THE 'ME' FACTOR.

Be gentle with *you* while making decisions and focus on making just one decision a day. You're going through a lot of changes and it's not unusual to experience high stress levels. Don't ignore them – go for a walk, take up yoga or meditate. See your family doctor for a checkup within the first two months after a loved one's death.

4. MAKE SOME CHANGES TO YOUR ENVIRONMENT.

Don't get stuck in the past. Redecorate a room, buy some new furniture or move around the old pieces. It won't take away the pain, but it'll help you make a fresh new start.

5. DON'T TAKE ADVICE PERSONALLY.

In making decisions, well-intentioned people can bombard you with advice. I was told that my house was too big to live in alone, when I should start dating, when I should return to work, etc. I didn't take any action until I was comfortable with my own decisions.

6. FOLLOW YOUR INTUITION.

Sometimes you have to take a chance when there's nothing but your intuition to guide you in making decisions. Even though my financial planner was recommended to me, I decided to choose him because I instinctively trusted him.

RESOURCES

1. *Why Keep It Secret*, published by the Ontario Blue Cross, is a brochure on how to file certain documents once a loved one has died. Contact the Ontario Blue Cross or check with your local library branch or financial planner.

2. *Do You Want To Make Money Or Fool Around?* by John Spooner (Adams Media Corporation, 2000)
John shares an invaluable collection of insights and proven strategies you can use to make and keep more money in the market.

3. Online resources, articles and fact sheets from AARP (formerly known as the American Association of Retired Persons). Check out the article, "Getting Legal Help" at **www.aarp.org/griefandloss/articles/72_a.html**.

CHAPTER 6

HOLIDAYS AND THEIR MEANING

Coping with the loss of a loved one is always difficult, but it's more so during special holidays, such as Christmas, anniversaries and birthdays. You'll probably find the usual feelings of grief and loneliness heightened during these special occasions. You will get through them, but it will take a lot of courage on your part and support on the part of family and friends. You may also find it helpful to change holiday traditions and rituals so the memories are less potent and painful.

As time goes on, your grief will change and mellow out, and the pain will subside within your heart and soul. You will, one day, be able to tolerate the holidays, but be gentle with yourself and recognize that the scars of grief you carry with you wouldn't have been there if you didn't love. I never thought I could face the holidays again after losing my loved ones, but I did. Here's my story.

ALL I WANTED FOR CHRISTMAS WAS...
MY FAMILY

How much did I love Christmas? I would start my Christmas shopping in July of each year! I was the social convener of the century, organizing party after party. And, of course, a real tree was mandatory. In fact, my collection of Christmas ornaments grew so large that I was running out of space to house them. There were Christmas ornaments with my children's names and ones we created together when the children were young.

I loved the smell of a Christmas tree and loved touching the needles. At our house, we would decorate the tree together as a family, listening to Christmas carols and drinking eggnog.

Death changed all that – at least at first. The pain in my heart was so huge, I wished I could go to sleep on the first day of December and wake up a month later. It was two years after my husband's death before I was able to even enter the menswear department at the store; every sweater, every shirt reminded me that I had no husband to buy for.

The sadness was so encompassing that even the hint of joy made me feel guilty – if I was letting go of grief, for even a second, was I also letting go of the memory of my lost loved ones?

I struggled with resentment, too. I found it very difficult to be around family and friends who were happy about the holidays. I spent the first Christmas after my husband, Rhod, died with my son and his family. They were excited about the holiday season, and my daughter-in-law had done a great job decorating the house and baking special treats. They had many gifts for me. Everyone tried to make it a typical Christmas, with the usual family traditions – as if nothing had changed. There was a pretense that everything was normal, that Rhod was just on holiday somewhere. He wasn't, and I was angry with him for leaving me and envied my son for his full family.

I realize now that my anger, resentment and guilt were all part of a normal grief process that is somehow heightened by holidays. I no longer struggle with those feelings. Of course I miss my loved ones most during the holidays, but I am thankful for the many holidays that I did share with them.

Prepare for the worst but hope for the best.

I would get all stirred up emotionally at least one month before a significant holiday. The first Christmas was difficult without Rhod but I put a lot of unnecessary stress on myself worrying about it. When it arrived, I got through it and I then realized it was the leading up to the event that was worst. Then I prepared myself for the next one a little better.

Creating New Traditions

AN END IS ALSO A NEW BEGINNING. INSISTING ON THE same rituals will not bring back the past; it will only serve to remind you of your loss. Begin again by creating new traditions and rituals for yourself.

Give yourself treats from your loved one.

For several birthdays, Valentine's Days and Christmases after Rhod died, I treated myself to a memorable gift. On the first birthday, I bought myself a pair of diamond earrings I had wanted before he died. I bought them from him and thanked him and remember him fondly when I wear them.

I started by approaching Christmas differently. I bought all new decorations for the tree, choosing a completely different colour scheme – gold and purple. I had fun putting on lots of angels on the tree with my grandchildren.

The family also coped that first Christmas by moving our

celebration to December 20. Then, on Christmas Day, I went out east to be with extended family. For the next few years we celebrated on Boxing Day. Changing the date seemed to take the emphasis off the holiday somehow and planning trips gave me something to look forward to.

Every year after Steven's death, Rhod and I went on a Caribbean holiday on December 26. When Rhod died, I could not go anymore. I tried the first year after Rhod died. My daughter and I went to the beautiful, tropical island of St. Maarten. But it was a difficult vacation for both of us. The sunshine and beaches did nothing to relieve the reminder of my usual travelling companion. I couldn't watch the sunset as all the happy couples cavorting on the beach enjoyed it. "Why me and not them?" I was angry and depressed – worse, I felt so guilty that I was bringing my daughter down with me.

The trip was a mistake, but a valuable one. I learned that in order to survive the holidays, I would have to change the way I celebrated them. From then on, Christmas would have to look very different from Christmases past.

On Steven's birthday, the first year after his death, many of his childhood friends came to my home and planted a maple tree in the backyard to honour his spirit. We celebrated his life by retelling the stories and reliving the memories.

Even now, on Steven's birthday, I relive his life and I take quiet time to go through the photos, to ponder fond memories and, briefly, consider regrets.

Memorialize your loved ones.

Keep your loved one's memory alive in special projects during the holidays. I donated to the Stained Glass Window Fund at our church in Rhod's memory and when I'm in church during significant events, it helps when I gaze up at this beautiful window and silently thank God for having Rhod in my life. Donating a poinsettia in a loved one's memory is healing too.

It won't be necessary to recreate holidays permanently. There will come a point in your grief journey when you will welcome time-honoured traditions again. For me, it was two long years after Rhod's death when I was able once again to enjoy Christmas parties, throwing myself into festivities with my usual vigour. Your time frame may be different from mine. There is no prescribed path or finite time frame.

The most important thing is to take the first step and maybe that step will take you in a new holiday direction.

Book a getaway on your birthday.

There's no reason why you need to be alone during your birthday, so take your mind off things. Rhod and I always celebrated our birthdays in a big way, so when he died this was a big void for me. On the years that I couldn't stay in town I planned a fun day away with my girlfriends so I wouldn't feel so lonely.

Think Outside the Self

FOCUSING ON THE NEEDS OF OTHERS WILL HELP YOU immensely during the holidays. Not only does it divert your natural preoccupation with grief, it also replaces feelings of powerlessness with feelings of purpose.

Shortly after Steven died, Rhod worked a Christmas-morning shift for a co-worker so he could go home and be with his young family. Rhod knew he gave this man and his family a great gift and it did not cost him anything – in fact, the good deed filled a little of Rhod's emptiness.

I have mentored a young widow for two years. Her husband died in an industrial accident after only a year of marriage, and now she was suicidal. After much persuasion, she agreed to go for a walk with me for an hour once or twice a week. It made a big difference during significant holidays. I shared the pain of suicide survivors like me, and she listened. Our walk, and talk, didn't make her pain go away, but I think the connection helped her – I know it helped me.

So volunteer at a soup kitchen. Invite an elderly senior for holiday dinner. Read books to children in the hospital over the holidays. Give someone else a break and you'll find that you get a grief break.

Understand the Pain of Holidays.

If we recognize that grief can carve us into better people, we will find it easier to embrace pain. Still, it will take time to go through myriad emotions necessary to get to this point. Start with acceptance. Special occasions will cause a surge of grief, an added vulnerability. But realize, as time moves on, that the surge will be brief and the space between pain will widen. Then, remember that you wouldn't have pain if you hadn't had love.

TAKE A GRIEF BREAK

GIVE YOURSELF PERMISSION TO TAKE A 'GRIEF BREAK' during the holidays – and make it a guilt-free break. Sometimes, that's as simple as making a conscious choice to step away from grieving and step toward joy – at least for a short time. Push your grief away, lock it in a closet. No, you're not avoiding it, just escaping from it during a particularly tough time. Make a pact with yourself, especially if you have young children, to mourn before and after a holiday, but not all the way through it.

Love the new you.

Grieving will be probably be the hardest work you'll ever have to do. Each loss will change you permanently. As time goes on for me, I look within me and feel a sense of pride on how far I have come in my journey. I can look in the mirror and tell myself that I am proud and that I love me.

∽ From My Journal ∽

December 22, 1999 – Another day. Feeling down, down, down. There's a void in my life. My heart is so heavy. I can't seem to catch my breath. I received a Christmas card yesterday from a friend and she wrote a note saying that she hoped time was healing my wound. I don't see this as a wound, but as an amputation. My heart and soul are gone forever.

February 14, 2000 – Valentine's Day. Damn. I'm angry today – with you, Rhod. I found one of your cards and I put it on the dining room table. You did buy me great cards. I'm glad I kept them.

April 6, 2002 – Would have been our wedding anniversary today. A very painful weekend. I relived our wedding day. I cried for hours. I feel better now. Maybe I'll go to the cemetery later.

Strategies: Holiday Survival Plan

Holidays can be stressful, so use this plan to make it through these particularly difficult times.

1. AVOID SHOPPING MALLS DURING HOLIDAYS.

I gave gift certificates and cash for Christmas gifts for the first few years. Shopping malls can be crazy with shoppers and you may find you just don't have the energy to be there.

2. SURROUND YOURSELF WITH FAMILY AND FRIENDS.

You will need extra support during the holidays.

3. LOWER EXPECTATIONS – OF YOURSELF AND OTHERS.

I felt very vulnerable, lonely and exhausted during special occasions so I did not force myself to go the extra mile as in previous years. Forget cards, cut back on shopping, cooking and baking. Decide what's really, truly important and spend your energy accordingly.

4. ALLOW OTHERS TO CARE FOR YOU.

Take off your 'entertainment director' hat and accept invitations from others. If you decide to host, delegate, delegate, delegate.

5. CHANGE YOUR RITUALS.

Celebrate the holiday before or after the date. At Christmas I donated money to the Victorian Order of Nurses on behalf of Rhod, Steven and Tate; their names are inscribed on a plaque, mounted on a memorial wall in our hometown. For their birthdays, I donate to the Trans Canada Trail – an environmental initiative that was important to my husband and son. If a loved one died from cancer, consider a donation to a cancer charity or any specific medical research organization.

6. SEEK SOLACE IN HIGHER POWERS.

Attend a church service, meditate, or spend time in nature. Find your own brand of spirituality. My church has a special service for people dealing with loss during the Christmas season.

7. HAVE A CANDLELIGHTING CEREMONY AT THE GRAVESITE.

On Steven's birthday, more than 20 family members and friends gathered at his gravesite. Rhod lit his candle and shared a memory with all of us. Then he lit mine and I shared a memory and so on until all of the candles were lit.

8. GET A MAKEOVER.

You will be feeling dull and sad during the holidays and it will show. Polishing up the exterior won't rid the pain you feel inside, but it will give you a lift. So treat yourself to a facial, pedicure or even a hair colour treatment.

RESOURCES

1. *The Art of Happiness: A Handbook For Living* by The Dalai Lama and Howard C. Cutler, MD (Riverhead Books, 1998)
Learn how to defeat anger, anxiety and discouragement and live a happy live despite suffering. This is an especially important message during the holidays.

2. *The Fall of Freddie the Leaf* by Lou Buscaglia, PhD (Henry Holt and Company, 1982)
This is a children's book suitable for all ages. It tells a story of Freddie and his companion and how their leaves change with the passing seasons. It illustrates the balance between life and death.

3. *Grief and the Holidays* by Doug Manning – Audio Cassette (In-Sight Books, 1995)
This tape is specifically designed for the bereaved coping with the difficulty of the holidays without their loved one(s).

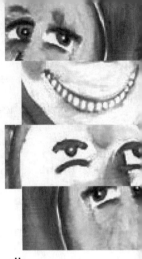

CHAPTER 7

CHILDREN
AND GRIEF

Death is a certainty in life. It happens all around us every day – we see it in the news, in nature, and sometimes at home through our pets and loved ones. Even though we'd like to shelter our children from its pain and anguish, death is something they can't escape. In fact, their experience with bereavement in their early years will affect how they view death and loss later in life.

Children need to feel comforted, supported and able to express their feelings about death.

In this chapter, we explore how children grieve following the death of a loved one and how we, as caregivers, can help them mourn a loss.

REMEMBERING DADDY AND GRANDPA

When I was growing up, death was a normal part of life. When a loved one died, he or she was 'waked' in the family home and more than likely in a room called a parlour. I recall as a young child of five years old going to my Aunt Maggie's funeral with my parents. At the visitation, I remember asking my dad to lift me up to see Aunt Maggie in her casket. It was not a scary experience for me because I had never been sheltered from death or the rituals that accompany it.

I lived in a small community in Newfoundland and everyone took part in funerals. It was natural for everyone to attend the visitations (deceased body in own home) and funerals (church) and later accompany family to the graveside committal (family and friends dug the grave and took part in lowering the casket and then covering the casket with earth). In fact, the families actually took part in cleansing the body and preparing it for burial. There may have been several generations living in a family home, so it wasn't rare for family members to witness both the birth and death of a loved one in the family home. My experience has helped me in my own grief and mourning process and, as a result, I'm comfortable talking about death with my children and grandchildren.

Don't shelter a child from the funeral experience.

Never force a child to go to the visitation or funeral, but give him the option to go and say goodbye to a loved one. Tell children in advance what they can expect and make sure you're right beside them to support them.

One of my clients (age 55) had unresolved issues surrounding her mom's death when her husband died. She was eight years old when her mother died and she was sent to stay with an aunt in another city. When she returned home a few days later, she was told by her father that her mother died.

Breaking the News

THE BIGGEST CHALLENGE WHEN INFORMING CHILDREN about death is showing them how comfortable you are in talking about it and dealing with it yourself.

As adults, we have a tendency to want to protect children from the experience of death but we are only protecting ourselves. Children want honesty and openness. Don't lie to children or use euphemisms about death to protect them. For example, don't say Daddy has passed away but Daddy has died. If you say Mommy is asleep, a child may think that Mommy is going to wake up again. I

Children can teach us about grief and mourning.

Children are often open about how they feel about a loved one's death. If they talk or cry openly about a death, let them. If you stop them, they may not reach out to you for support and, instead, get the message that it isn't okay to show emotion. Validate the child's feelings and offer lots of comforting hugs and support.

once counselled a little boy named Billy (age 7) who, after being told his mother was sleeping but didn't wake up, was afraid to go to sleep at night because he thought he was going to die too. Once I explained death to him, he was able to sleep with a Mickey Mouse (his favourite cartoon character) night light. Eight months later, he didn't need the security of the night light.

When my son Steven died, his daughter, Lyndsay, was only 18 months old. She didn't understand the concept of death when she was told that Daddy died, but she seemed to sense that things had changed around her. When she attended one of the visitations and the funeral, I remember Lyndsay saying to me "Daddy asleep" as

Don't be afraid to tell a child the cause and circumstances of death.

Children will find out about the circumstance of death at some point and, often, when they do, they may be misinformed if you don't tell them yourself. The wrong information may be harmful and complicate the grief journey.

she viewed him in his casket. Even at her young age, I tried to reinforce the importance of being honest, so I'd often repeat to her that "Daddy died." (See the sidebar, "Q & As for Children" on page 146 on using appropriate language.)

When my husband died, Lyndsay was eight years old, and our other grandchildren, Mckinlay and Tristan, were eight months old and nearly three years old respectively. They were told that Rhod was very ill and Lyndsay wanted to know if he was going to die. I answered her very honestly – "I didn't know for sure, but he was very sick."

Before the funeral, I remember telling the children that Grandpa's body stopped working; he couldn't move his fingers or his toes, he couldn't breathe or snore and he would not be alive again but would live in our hearts.

Tell a child immediately about the death of a loved one.

Don't wait for a child to hear the news from someone else. If you prepare them earlier, they'll be able to cope with the news better and not complicate their feelings with anger.

In addition to giving the children our support, we used other aids to help them come to terms with their loss, such as playing the movie *The Lion King*. It later became their favourite movie and helped them validate their feelings.

When my grandchildren came to visit me months later, I encouraged them to share their memories of Grandpa when they told me how much they missed him. Tristan told me how much he loved going to play in the park with Grandpa. Lyndsay missed Grandpa lifting her up in his arms so she could touch the ceiling.

In the following years, Tristan and Mckinlay (now ages 6 and 8) experienced other deaths, including their beloved Poppa Kelch, who assumed the role of both Grandpas after Rhod died. Their initial experience with death, in addition to our honesty and openness, has lessened their fear and anxiety about death.

Understanding Suicide

LYNDSAY WAS TOO YOUNG TO UNDERSTAND DEATH, especially suicide, when her father took his own life. It wasn't until she was about six years old that she seemed to understand the concept of suicide. That's when she also learned about the true details of her father's death while overhearing a conversation that her mother was having with a friend. To 'protect' Lyndsay, her mother told her years earlier that her father died in a car accident. Lyndsay, who was very angry with her mom for not telling her the truth, started to ask questions about the circumstances around his death and later had to be told the truth.

Notify a child's school about the death of a loved one.

A child's teacher can provide additional support in the weeks following a death. For example, my grandson, Tristan, was able to talk openly with his teacher and peers about his grandfather's death (Poppa Kelch) and shared his memories of him by bringing photos to school.

At such a young age, she was worried that she had caused his death.

When she was eight years old and her grandfather died, a lot of buried feelings resurfaced, especially the feelings of guilt about her dad's death. Again she questioned whether she had done something wrong to cause his death. I reassured her that she was not the cause of Steven's death and that his death happened because he was depressed and unhappy, although not all depressed people take their own life. I explained that her dad had a very quiet personality and that he buried a lot of his feelings and that, in contrast, it was comforting to hear her share her feelings with me. I tried to also emphasize that it was natural for her to grieve her dad's loss now that Grandpa died.

Be aware that a child may be suffering multiple losses.

A loved one's death can mean a new family home, new neighbourhood and a new school. So, be sure to offer a child extra support during all his adjustments.

BUILDING MEMORIES

BECAUSE LYNDSAY WAS SO YOUNG WHEN HER FATHER died, she did not have any memories of him. I helped her with her grief by sharing my memories of Steven through personal stories, photos and videotapes. She came to know her dad through my eyes. I told her how much he loved her, how he played with her, sang songs and read stories to her, and how he was so proud of her. I told her stories of his childhood and teenage years over and over again. I remember when she became fascinated with watching a video of when she was baptized because Steven was often holding her and laughing with her.

Accept help for your child.

You're grieving your loved one too and may need a break from typical family chores. Call in your support network at this time to help you with household chores, babysitting needs, etc. Besides, it's healthy for children to spend time with cousins at a sleepover as my grandchildren did to give their parents a break.

To keep that memory fresh, I made her a copy of the video on her sixth birthday.

As I shared more of my memories with Lyndsay, she wanted to know more about her father. And she always came equipped with lots of 'why' questions. "Why did he leave me if he loved me? Why didn't he stay around and see me grow up?" She was convinced that her life would have been different if he was alive. I kept reminding her that he would live in our hearts and that he left us a very special gift (she resembles him in looks and personality).

Recently Lyndsay (she's now 14) told me how much she missed her dad and how she feels cheated that she did not get to know him. She is saddened that he won't be around for her Grade 8 graduation this next year, or her high-school graduation or any other graduation, and that she feels like there's a big part of her life missing. I reassured her that what she was feeling was normal. Even though I was waiting for a special time in her life to give her the rest of her dad's mementos, she's convinced me that the time was now. I had kept a book with all of Steven's school records, from kindergarten to high school, which I'm passing on to her. It's also the time to give her the model schooner Steven carved with his hands and other special treasures that will help her build her own memories of her dad and better deal with her loss. It is time once again to review more old movies with Lyndsay. On her 14th birthday, I gave Lyndsay a portfolio of Steven's college architectural drawings and she was thrilled. She told me it was the best gift she had ever received. She wasted no time going through them and commented on her father's handwriting.

Honesty is the best policy.

Be open and honest with children. Children are afraid of what they don't know and not of what they know. When they ask questions about death, answer them honestly. If you don't have an answer, tell them so. If you have trouble talking to a child about a particular death, get help from someone who is comfortable talking about it.

Age-Appropriate Reactions

When talking about a death, it's important to use age-appropriate language for each child. Keep in mind that a child's reaction will vary with his personal experience.

Infant to age 2: Exhibiting behaviours such as thumb-sucking, crying more than usual, biting, hitting. The loss of a primary caregiver is threatening to them.

My granddaughter Lyndsay was 18 months old when my son Steven died. She began to wake up during the night and cry for her mommy and daddy. She also ate very little and, in general, fussed a lot.

Ages 3-6: These children may be afraid of losing another loved one. They need reassurance that they are loved and will be cared for. I often suggest children hold their favourite teddy bear when they are afraid. It's important to help a child put a name to these feelings, for example, sadness, numbness, anger, grief, etc. They may have a tendency to ask questions about the death over and over again and require honest answers. They may also re-enact death in their play.

In this age group, children may show regressive behaviours, such as clinging to parents, thumb-sucking, losing potty training skills or resorting to baby talk. My grandchildren Mckinlay and Tristan, for example, wanted to sleep with their parents for some time after their grandfathers died.

One of my seven-year-old clients was having nightmares about losing her mom and her sisters in a car accident after her father died. She would wake up from these nightmares only to discover that she had wet the bed. We worked on her emotions through artwork. Several months later, her nightmares diminished and the bedwetting lessened.

Ages 6-11: These children, especially 10- to 11-year-olds, may have a clearer understanding of death. They realize that death is final and that Mommy or Daddy is gone forever. They may be socially and scholastically impaired. These children also express their grief through play and/or through arts and crafts, which are beneficial. They may act out because they don't know how to handle these new feelings of grief. They need to vent their frustrations through a support group or sports.

Ages 12 and up: They understand cognitively about death but may not be able to grasp the spiritual aspect. They may act out, withdraw from activities or believe life is unfair. They may also search for the meaning of life by questioning whether there really is a heaven or an afterlife. Acting out or withdrawing are normal behaviours for a teen, but get help if a teen harms himself or others, or withdraws for long periods. They need openness, patience and understanding to express their grief.

One of my clients (age 12) came to me a year after her father's death. She was usually angry and isolated herself in her bedroom. She often picked fights at school and was grounded for her behaviour. She also thought her father's death (suicide) had something to do with her. Once she was assured that there was nothing she could have done to prevent his death, she was able to focus on good memories of her father.

∼ From My Journal ∼

March 20, 1999 – Lyndsay (age 8) and I went through some photos of my holidays with Rhod. We put them in albums, laughed and shared memories of Grandpa. I also shared stories about her father. She is so much like him. She told me that she loves Grandpa's blanket. She said that she wasn't going to wash it because she could still see, smell and feel Grandpa around it.

April 10, 1999 – Tristan is enjoying the photo album of Rhod that I gave him. He takes it to bed with him every night and sometimes hides it from his sister.

March 12, 2003 – This is Tristan's seventh birthday. Mckinlay (age 5) came over today carrying an empty photo album and said that Tristan was sad yesterday. She said, "Tristan misses Grandpa." I asked her if she wanted me to fill her album with photos of Grandpa and she said yes. She chose the photos that she wanted and then we placed them in the album. She laughed and said, "Now I have my own pictures and I can look at them and remember Grandpa. I know he is in heaven looking down on us."

RELATIONSHIPS AND GRIEF

Children will naturally grieve differently depending on their relationship with a deceased. Even then, each child has a unique style of grieving, depending on prior death experiences, age of the child, his or her support network, nature of the death, the unique characteristics of the loved one who died, and cultural and ethnic background of the child.

Don't minimize non-familial relationships. Little Johnny may have been close to a neighbour he visited often and now he is upset that he has died. On the flipside, his grandmother may have lived 3,000 kilometres away and he only saw her every few years. He didn't have an attachment to her and didn't express the same sadness when she died. Both relationships are different. Like adults, children will grieve those individuals that they have bonded with and not necessarily only people who are part of their family tree.

Q & As for Children

Use simple language when communicating death to young children. Here are some common questions and appropriate answers you can use.

Q What is dead?

A Dead is when the body is no longer working. Grandpa can't breathe, move his fingers, laugh, talk or walk anymore.

Q What is a funeral?

A A funeral is when family and friends get together to say goodbye to the person who died.

Q What is a burial?

A A burial is when the body, which is inside a casket, is placed into the ground or a special place in a wall.

Q What is a casket?

A A special box for burying a dead body.

Q What is a cemetery?

A A cemetery is a place where bodies are buried.

Q What is a funeral home?

A It is a place where bodies are kept until the body is buried. This is the place where family and friends can come to visit and say their goodbyes.

Q What is a grave?

A A grave is a hole in the ground where the body is buried in the cemetery.

Q What is cremation?

A Cremation is when the body is reduced to small pieces of bone by heat.

Q What is an obituary?

A An obituary is a short article in the newspaper that talks about the person who died.

Q What is a viewing?

A A viewing is when people come to see the person who died.

Q Where are Grandma's feet?

A In the casket. (You may have to show the child.)

Q What is suicide?

A Suicide is when a person takes his/her own life.

Parents FYI

Q Should a child be told that the loved one died of suicide?

A Yes, it's important to be honest and open. You may have to reassure the child time and time again that they were not responsible for the death.

Danger Grief Signals

Some children may feel guilty for a loved one's death because they 'wished' it once. Or they may have trouble dealing with their grief. If some of the following signs persist or increase in intensity long after a death, your child may need counselling to deal with his or her emotions. You might also consider getting counselling, too, to help your child work through the grief. Here are some signals to watch for:

~ If the child does not accept (denies) that a loved one died.

~ If the child is having panic attacks and fears going to bed at night or gets upset when a parent leaves the room.

~ If the child is experiencing many physical symptoms, such as a tummy ache or headache, without just cause after being examined by a family physician.

~ If the child has feelings of guilt that continue long after the death.

~ If the child has personality changes long after the death. For example, if an easy-going, personable child becomes withdrawn, introverted or constantly angry.

~ If the child spends all of his/her time isolated from family and friends.

~ If the child is acting out behaviours excessively and harming him/herself or others.

~ If a child is resorting to alcohol or drugs to try to suppress the pain of loss.

Myths about Children and Grieving

1. Children's grief is structured and predictable.

No two children will grieve the same. Some may be quiet and won't express their feelings as freely; others will be more expressive about how they feel.

2. Younger children, especially infants and toddlers, are too young to grieve and mourn.

If younger children are capable of giving and receiving love then they will grieve and mourn, too.

3. Children shouldn't attend funerals.

It's important for children to attend funerals because it encourages adults and children to support each other and to honour the loved one who died. However, it's important not to force a child to go to a funeral. Prepare the child before attending a funeral by explaining what takes place in clear, simple language.

4. Children shouldn't see the dead body.

Children will often ask to go see Grandma in her casket. Often, a child's curiosity will prompt them to take the initiative. It's a good idea that you accompany the child when visiting the casket.

5. When children grieve once, then their grief should be over and done with.

Children will re-grieve their losses in light of new knowledge and abilities as they grow and develop.

Strategies: Helping Children with Grief

Here are some ways to help children express their feelings and cope with the loss of a loved one.

1. ARM YOURSELF WITH TOOLS TO HELP A CHILD DEAL WITH GRIEF.

It's important to learn about the grief and mourning process so you're better able to deal with changes and prepare your family. Attend seminars on grief, surf the Internet and access the library at your local funeral home.

2. PLANT A FLOWER GARDEN TOGETHER.

Gardening is very healing, so get your child involved in it. Take a child shopping and buy your loved one's favourite plant or flower and then make a garden or plant flowers together at the cemetery.

3. FIND A GRIEF BUDDY FOR YOUR CHILD.

Children need to express their feelings and know that they are not alone. Befriending a child of the same age with similar losses will help the child cope with his or her loss. My granddaughter Mckinlay (age 6 at the time) came into one of my sessions with two of my clients (ages 5 and 7). I gave them the task of doing some creative artwork and then expressing their story to me.

4. BUY A JOURNAL FOR YOUR CHILD.

Journaling is a very healthy vent for grief. Best of all, it's suitable for children of all ages. Younger children can draw pictures and when they are older can write their feelings. I've been buying my granddaughter Lyndsay a diary every year since she was five years old (she's now 14).

5. **Give a child a framed photo of the deceased loved one.**

Go through the family albums with the child and let him choose a special photo and then put it in a special frame so it'll remind him that his loved one will always be with him. My grandchildren Tristan and Mckinlay would say goodnight to their grandpa when they looked at his picture before they went to sleep.

6. **Send a gift basket to the child.**

Children are the forgotten mourners and we often neglect their feelings. Prepare a basket for the child with crayons, art materials, colouring books and comfort foods.

7. **Realize that grief is a process, not an event.**

Grief is a journey and children need to express their feelings of loss over time. As they adjust to the loss of a loved one, they may have many outbursts of grief. Don't rush them through this process. Instead, nurture them with lots of love and be a good role model.

8. **Involve a child in sports or some form of physical activity.**

A child may need to occupy himself and use up pent-up energy for something productive. Sign her up for soccer, hockey, baseball, or another sport of interest.

RESOURCES

1. *Healing the Grieving Child's Heart. 100 Practical Ideas For Families, Friends and Caregivers* by Alan D. Wolfelt, PhD (Companion Press, 2000)
An excellent guide to help caregivers facilitate and encourage the mourning process for children.

2. *Aardy Aardvark Finds Hope* by Donna O'Toole (Rainbow Productions, 1988)
This is a story about animal loss and the eventual hope for healing.

3. *Memory Book: For Bereaved Children* by Kathleen Braza (Healing Resources, 1988)
A workbook to encourage children to draw and write about their grief. Ages 5 to 11.

4. *Grover* by Vera and Bill Cleaver (Lippincott, 1970)
A story about the process of accepting a mother's suicide, a death she chose over her impending death from cancer. Ages 10 to 14.

5. *Helping Children Grieve and Grow: A Guide For Those Who Care* by Donna O'Toole with Jerre Corry (Compassion Books, 1998)
This booklet is designed for the caregiver to learn more about how children experience loss and grief and what you, as an adult, can do to help.

6. *Love You Forever* by Robert Munsch (Firefly Books Ltd., 1986)
He tells the story about everlasting love between a mother and child.

7. *Forever In My Heart* by Jennifer Levine (Mt. Rainbow Publications, 1992)
A workbook for children anticipating the death of a terminally ill parent.

8. *I Know Someone Who Has Died* by Connie Manning (In-Sight Books, Inc., 1998)
A colouring book to facilitate the grieving process for young children.

CHAPTER 8

REDISCOVERING
INTIMACY

We all know that death is an inevitable, natural part of the life cycle. But to think that we will outlive our spouse can be difficult to imagine. We push these fears aside even though we likely have family members, friends or colleagues who are widowed. Like any other death, the loss of a spouse can cripple us, but what's more, it can leave us feeling isolated, lonely, and robbed of our identity and intimacy in a relationship.

When my husband Rhod died, I lost the second half to a strong, intimate relationship. In the months and years that followed, I struggled to come to terms with his death and later to find intimacy once again. Then, one day, I found love again. I never thought it would happen again, but it did and it can happen to you too.

TILL DEATH DO US PART

Rhod and I had known each other since we were children. From the time he was nine years old and I was seven, we already seemed destined to spend our lives together. Everyone teased us because our names rhymed – Audrey and Rhodri.

A t a young age (I was 17 and Rhod, 19), we were married, and soon after, parents to three children. We were married for 31 years before Rhod's death in 1999 and, together, we experienced many struggles and joys like any other couple. What made our marriage so successful despite our marrying young was honest and open communication.

We often leaned on each other in desperate times, such as when our son Steven and our granddaughter Tate died. But when Rhod died I was alone. My main support was gone and I was afraid, isolated and lonely. Our healthy, intimate relationship was gone in an instant.

Time didn't seem to make a difference in healing my pain – once the shock wore off after his death, the pain of his loss became more intense and the loneliness sometimes became unbearable. For the first couple of months, I kept telling myself that he was on vacation and that he would be coming home soon. When the phone or doorbell rang, I often imagined it was Rhod. I knew that in my heart he had died but I couldn't accept it. I often wondered if I could survive without him in my life.

Don't be afraid to love again.

Losing a spouse is a very difficult grief journey. While the price of loving is grief when a loved one dies, take comfort that you can find happiness again. Think of the opportunity as a second chance at being in a relationship with a special someone.

I was a single person now living in a 'couples' world. While my family and friends continued to show me their love, I missed the love and intimacy that I shared with my husband. I often felt like I didn't belong to anyone anymore and that my role in life was confusing – I was no longer a wife, a lover, a confidante or companion. My self-worth was now shattered with his loss and I had to redefine who I was in life.

Losing Rhod also had many secondary losses – I lost a confidant, a lover and a best friend. I enjoyed satisfying and supporting Rhod in many ways, especially during the growth of his career, making nurturing meals for him, listening to him express his feelings, making love, and assuring him unconditionally that I was always there for him.

Be responsible for your own happiness.

Be happy with who you are as a person first and look after your own needs. Only after I took care of me did I consider finding new love as a bonus.

In turn, he supported me in reaching my career goals. For example, when I went to university, Rhod assumed some additional household responsibilities, such as grocery shopping and cooking several meals a week. He also continued to be my main cheerleader and told me that he was proud of me.

Throughout our life together, Rhod and I loved to travel together, attend plays and, on the spur of the moment, try to get tickets to our favourite concerts, such as Neil Diamond. Physically, Rhod expressed his love for me with lots of hugs and kisses. I missed his body next to mine in bed. I missed having conversations with him and eating meals together.

Be specific about your needs.

When you're ready to take the plunge in the dating scene again, make a list of what you want in a relationship. Are you ready to settle down or maybe play the field for a while? Are you looking for companionship or passion or both? Don't be with someone for the sake of not being alone.

Moving Ahead

RHOD AND I HAD BOTH AGREED LONG BEFORE HIS DEATH that we wanted each other to carry on, enjoy life fully and find another partner should one of us die. Our agreement made me feel more comfortable once I was ready for an intimate relationship.

Even so, I couldn't imagine loving or being loved by another man for the first couple of years after Rhod's death. I was also scared of loving someone and then losing them as I did Rhod. My wounds were very deep, and I couldn't take that chance to suffer another loss.

Enjoy the dating game.

No matter what your age, you'll get a charge out of dating again. If you're nervous about dating, think about it as meeting new people and learning from their experiences. Dating will also boost your self-esteem and confidence. Make it a dinner date or a play or somewhere fun. You know you're healing when you accept that first invitation from a member of the opposite sex.

At first, I took the edge off my loneliness for Rhod by letting my cats (P-2 and Coco) sleep on my bed for 18 months. Two little warm bodies (one lying at my feet and the other at my back) gave me the comfort I needed. I also found comfort in holding and cuddling a teddy bear that my co-workers gave me when Rhod was in the hospital.

Take charge of your own intimacy.

You're responsible for your own intimacy needs. Once you realize this, you'll be less stressed and lonely. Taking charge means learning to enjoy your own body, whether it's through manual stimulation or other forms. Masturbation is an act of self-love. It's important to remember that any way we feed and nurture ourselves helps us on the road to healing. In the safety of your home, feel free to give yourself what you need.

Even though sex was the furthest thing from my mind after Rhod died, I was forced to deal with it early on. (While sex is an integral part of a relationship, it becomes a taboo topic when a spouse dies.) But it's not what you might think. The physical act of sex was not only a way of expressing my love for Rhod, but it was a wonderful stress releaser for me. Three months after my husband died, my body began telling me it missed sex. My uterus began having spasms and contractions that prompted me to contact my gynecologist, who is also a sex therapist. What he told me shocked me – that the spasms in my uterus were happening because I had been sexually active for more than 30 years and now was sexually inactive. I wasn't interested in a relationship, let alone a sexual relationship, so my doctor encouraged me to pleasure myself through manual stimulation, something that was as foreign to me as a new language. I took his advice and found my own intimacy to be a tension reliever.

While the physical act had been partly addressed, I was still having a difficult time dealing with the emotional void Rhod's death left. I did a lot of soul-searching and knew I needed the time to nurture me before I could think about a new relationship with another man.

By the one-year mark, I was exploring the idea of another relationship and trying to imagine what it would be like. But I still wasn't emotionally ready.

I still thought about Rhod all the time. I kept reviewing our life together and wasn't ready to let it go. During this time, I planned for the future and set some goals, such as continuing my education, starting a private practice in grief counselling and taking early retirement from my workplace; but I made no plans to meet someone else.

Being involved in a relationship with someone else wouldn't be fair to the other person if my mind and spirit weren't committed.

Gather your warmth from other sources.

If your spouse was a source of comfort at nighttime, find other objects to keep you warm. Have a hot cup of tea or milk before bedtime, wrap yourself in extra blankets or cuddle up with furry friends or a teddy bear. I wore one of Rhod's favourite shirts to bed for the first few weeks after his death.

Still, I missed the physical touch of an intimate relationship too. So much so that I hugged everyone I came into contact with and did not want to let them go. Finally, I went to a massage therapist regularly for two years after Rhod's death. It helped me relax, and the physical touch from another human being was calming.

As time went on I became more independent and self-sufficient, and enjoyed living alone. I was only accountable to me and I knew that I would live on my own for a few years before making the decision to settle down with another partner.

Throw out the dowdiness and turn on your sensuality.

Don't neglect your physical appearance because you're grieving. Take control and take pride in your physical appearance. Nourish your sensual side by taking a bubble bath, lighting scented candles and reading a romance novel or listening to passionate music. Get a makeover. Looking good on the outside will help you feel better on the inside.

A New Relationship

FINDING A COMPATIBLE PARTNER WAS DIFFICULT AT FIRST because well-meaning friends and family kept trying to push me into relationships I knew wouldn't work. And when I began dating, many men wanted an intimate relationship even though it wasn't what I wanted. At the time, my daughter was happy to see me out on dates; my son was more reserved, even though today he tells me he's happy seeing me happy.

Then, 18 months after Rhod's death, I fell into a relationship laced in lust with a charming

Don't promote your spouse to sainthood.

You need to see your loved one as a whole person with all his strengths and limitations, in other words, as a real, perfectly flawed human being. In the beginning of my grief journey, I couldn't bring myself to think about the things that annoyed and frustrated me about Rhod. I realized that the "picture perfect dream" was comforting but it was more harmful in the end because if I got involved with another man, he could never measure up to my expectations.

man. His attention and compliments showered my ego, and the sexual intimacy made me feel more vibrant and alive. I likened the experience to waking up from a deep sleep. But after six months, I broke it off because I didn't want to settle down.

I continued to date other men but not commit to a relationship until I started seeing Brian again. I had dated him three

FINDING SEXUAL SPARKS

Your sexual interest may diminish or be nonexistent for many months after your loved one has died. How soon your sexual appetite returns depends on how you nourish yourself and the relationships that you experience in months and years to come. As my lust for life revived, so did my appetite for all things life-affirming and pleasurable. I didn't rush into a sexual relationship but sought after other expressions of feeling sensual and loved. For example, I frequently enjoyed a luxurious bath, body massage, reflexology and warm bear hugs, to name a few.

years after Rhod died but I wasn't ready for a relationship then. We started dating again in April 2003 and he is now the love of my life. I thank God for giving me a second chance at love.

I cherish the memories I had with Rhod and greatly appreciate our time together. I see aspects of my relationship with Brian that are not only different, but sometimes better because I now give myself the freedom to discover and develop new things. For example, Brian has introduced me to the world of auctions, classic cars and sports. Today, I look forward to creating new memories with Brian.

Give yourself permission to be a child again.

Think of your grieving journey as a young child learning how to walk for the first time. There will be times when you'll need to pull yourself up using some kind of support or get up over and over again after falling. But as the months pass, you'll take tiny steps, regain your balance and walk slowly. Soon you'll be taking confident strides.

UNDRESSING YOUR HAND

"Take this ring as a sign of my love"…it's those meaningful words you remember when looking at a wedding band, in addition to all the memories you've created over the years of marriage. It's no wonder some find it very difficult to remove a wedding ring from their finger.

Removing a wedding band is a sign that you are healing and ready to move on. Follow your intuition when deciding when to remove it. Start by practicing to take the ring off, maybe for one day to see how you feel. Monitor your self-esteem when you're not wearing your wedding band. Once you've decided to remove your rings, give them new purpose or meaning in the following ways:

~ Wear your rings on a chain around your neck.

~ Plan to give them to your children or grandchildren at a significant age. I gave my daughter, Lexine, my wedding ring and my son Gavin his father's wedding band.

~ Create a newly designed ring for your loved ones with your spouse's and/or your bands. I made my engagement ring into a pinkie ring that I plan to give to my granddaughter Lyndsay when she is 16.

WHEN IS IT OKAY TO HAVE AN INTIMATE RELATIONSHIP AGAIN?

There's a misconception that there's a set time frame when it's okay to be involved in another relationship after the death of a spouse. That time frame is personal and depends largely on you and your comfort with intimacy.

There are other factors that will determine how ready your are for intimacy, including: the relationship you had with your deceased spouse; the circumstances of your spouse's death (whether he/she was ill for a number of years or died suddenly); whether you have children at home; your financial stability; your support network; and other factors that are individual to you and your circumstances.

But it's important not to jump into a relationship because you are lonely. Some people marry or live with a new love too soon and later regret the decision. For me, I had to rediscover who I was after my husband's death and, over time, I realized that my happiness depended on me first and foremost. Once I welcomed a new relationship, I didn't head into it expecting someone else to make me happy.

Time frames are individual and unique, as these examples show:

- When my sister Doreen's husband died, she took her rings off three months later. She isn't currently in a relationship, but welcomes the possibility.

- When Denis (age 59) lost his wife, he was ready for an intimate relationship just months after her death. She was ill for six years before her death and Denis was her around-the-clock caregiver for five years until he accepted support from organizations in the community. He remarried a year later and is very happy.

- Chuck's (age 45) wife died after a two-year illness and he became intimate six months later. The relationship ended several months later. Three years later, he realized that he became involved with this woman too soon. He missed the touching, hugging and sexual contact after his wife died.

- Judy's (age 42) husband died after an 18-month illness. Judy began a relationship six months later with a family friend and is very happy.

- Phil's (age 58) spouse died suddenly in a car crash. He remarried less than one year after his wife's death. His grown children were upset with him and became resentful. His second marriage ultimately ended in divorce. He hadn't dealt with the trauma of his first wife's death and needed to mourn her loss before committing to another relationship.

From My Journal

September 24, 1999 – I went to a social function with my daughter and her family today. Everyone told me how great I looked. I'm good at fooling people...they have no idea the pain I'm feeling inside. A couple of people asked me if I was getting on with my life (whatever that meant!). I'm trying to survive without Rhod! Another lady asked if I would be interested in dating soon. She was only trying to be helpful, but I felt sad and hoped that her husband did not die soon.

July 30, 2000 – The loneliness within me is so deep at times it takes my breath away. It is difficult to believe that it is nearly 18 months since Rhod died. Someone once told me that the second year was more difficult than the first year. I tend to agree. The tears don't flow as frequently as the first year but when the tears flow, the wound is opened with such a force, and the feeling that I will never heal completely overwhelms me.

August 6, 2000 – Eighteen months today since Rhod died. I feel a sense of peace today (it started within me a couple of days ago). A feeling of reconciliation came over me when I went to bed and I prayed to Rhod for another connection with another partner...not necessarily permanent but someone to touch my life and give me hope.

How Can Spousal Loss Bereavement Groups Help?

If you're a group-oriented person, you may benefit from a widow/bereavement support group. They generally last between six to 10 weeks for one to two hours per session. A facilitator typically leads the group (usually six to12 persons dealing with loss) to talk about their loss and how it has affected their life. In this setting, you'll be with a group of people who are experiencing similar losses so you won't feel so alone and isolated. Sharing your story and listening to others tell their stories will help you form a common bond with others and, possibly, help develop long-lasting friendships.

My home church (Grace United) has a support group for widows coping with their loss. Other support groups, which usually aren't specific to spousal loss, may be provided by a funeral home. For information about joining a bereavement group, check your local newspaper, churches, bereavement network association, hospice or funeral home.

Strategies: Finding Intimacy

There are several ways to reconnect with yourself and boost your confidence. Try some of the following.

1. REACH OUT FOR COMFORTING HUGS.

Hugs are important in your healing. Even if you're not a hugger, learn to accept hugs. I was touch deprived and I reached out to family and friends when greeting them, and it gave me an extra boost.

2. FULFILL A DREAM.

Look at this time in your life as an opportunity to live unrequited dreams. Mike always loved the arts, and after his spouse died, he often went to the opera and theatre, and learned ballroom dancing. He not only fulfilled his dream of learning more about the arts, but it helped him cope with his loss. He later met his soulmate.

3. CHANGE YOUR SLEEPING ARRANGEMENTS.

Be in control of your bedroom and make it yours. If your spouse died at home (bedroom), you may have trouble falling asleep, so make the guest room your bedroom for a couple of weeks, or rearrange the furniture in your bedroom.

When Rhod died, I shopped for a new comforter and drapes for my bedroom.

4. TAKE CONTROL OF YOUR VOCABULARY.

Every time I said "I" instead of "we" I was reminded of my loss, but over time I accepted it. Saying "I" instead of "we" will help you feel empowered, so don't feel guilty about saying it.

5. TAP INTO YOUR SENSUAL SIDE.

You have to look after *you* now. So make a pleasure to-do list by exploring the things that give you most pleasure and help you feel sensual again. I enjoy the scent of lavender, so I sprayed it in my bedroom before I went to bed at night. I also made a ritual of having a decadent piece of chocolate (which I once read was a substitute for sex) with my cup of tea every afternoon. And I took belly-dancing lessons for six months — not only great exercise but lots of fun.

6. LEARN TO VALUE YOUR FREEDOM.

Your life has changed completely, but focus on its pluses. For example, you're now accountable to *you* and only you. My friend Monica enjoyed the luxury of sleeping late in the morning. When she went shopping, she didn't have to rush home to cook dinner.

RESOURCES

1. *How to Survive the Loss of a Love* by Melba Colgrove, PhD, Harold H. Bloomfield, MD, and Peter McWilliams (Prelude Press, 1976)
This book was given to me by one of my yoga students whose husband died. It's an easy-to-read book combined with poetry and tips on how to cope and survive loss.

2. *For Women Who Grieve: Embracing Life After the Death of Your Partner* by Tangea Tansley (Crossing Press, 1990)
This book, written in a down-to-earth tone, is full of practical advice. It not only deals with the legal and financial aspects of your loss, as well as the grief of family and friends, but also how to rediscover your own sexuality.

3. *Men & Grief: A Guide for Men Surviving the Death of a Loved One: A Resource for Caregivers and Mental Health Professionals* By Carol Staudacher (New Harbinger Publications, Inc., 1991)
I first used this book as a resource in the 1990s during my career training. It helped me understand Rhod's grief journey when our son Steven and granddaughter Tate died.

4. Sex In The City
My friend Becky introduced me to this hit TV series, now running in syndication. She would tape it weekly and we would get together at her house to watch this program about four single women in New York City and their sexual relationships. I not only had fun watching it but gained more confidence in my own sexuality.

5. comeasyouare.com
This website provides easy access to purchase sexual aids in the privacy of your own home. I first read about this site in a *Chatelaine* magazine article in 2002. I have since recommended the site to several of my friends and clients.

Additional websites for sexual aids:
www.goodvibes.com   www.grandopening.com

CHAPTER 9

FINDING STRENGTH IN FAITH AND SPIRITUALITY

Throughout life, we all acquire certain beliefs and values, which continually influence our decision-making. Our beliefs and values, then, become the foundation for our spiritual or religious beliefs and vice-versa. When a loved one dies, these beliefs can be challenged or strengthened because it may cause us to question everything that we've learned throughout our lives. Your life may seem unfair, you may feel lost and alone and you may feel like you've been unjustly 'targeted.' This chapter will focus on how I turned to my faith and spirituality to help me heal from the loss of loved ones.

HOW FAITH BECAME MY COMPANION

Religion played a significant role throughout my life. I was raised as a Protestant and, as a child, regularly attended church. Later in my teens, and again as a young parent, I taught Sunday (Bible) classes.

Every Sunday as a teen, I remember sitting around the kitchen table with my parents while we listened to a one-hour radio program by evangelist Billy Graham. And, I couldn't escape the insanely religious sermons by my Uncle George (my dad's brother), whom we would often visit as a family. During the entire visit, he often gave informal sermons, quoting the Bible in his booming voice and bouncing from his rocking chair as he yelled, "Hallelujah, praise the Lord!" Even though not all my experiences with religion were comforting, they helped me develop a strong belief in my God.

From an early age, I was also taught to fear God – I learned that he was all-powerful and a supreme being that I was never to question. To do anything against Protestant values and morals meant that my parents would not only punish me, but God would judge me in the afterlife. With this belief system in place, my seven siblings and I were always obedient and respected our parents. Family time was essential. So was the regular ritual of prayer, which we practiced at every meal time and before bedtime, kneeling beside our beds, hands folded in prayer reciting, "Now I lay me down to sleep. I pray the Lord my soul to keep and if I die before I wake, I pray the Lord my soul to take." These practices helped me acquire the knowledge and comfort that death was a part of our life cycle and, therefore, I didn't fear death.

TESTING FAITH

WHEN MY SON STEVEN DIED, MY FAITH GREW STRONGER.
I prayed to God every day to give my family the strength
to deal with his death. The year before his death, I was
already taking courses in world religions, such as
Christianity, Buddhism, Hinduism and Islam, to better
appreciate the cultures and faiths of many of the bereaved I
worked with in the palliative
care field. I became even
more passionate about these
studies after Steven's death. I
found comfort and strength in
studying the works of Thomas
Merton, Sam Keen, Karl Rahner
and James F. White, to name a
few. These studies, along with
one of my compassionate

Embrace your spiritual pain.

When we experience spiritual
pain, we can feel an inward
feeling of losing control, like
being lost in the 'wilderness'
and a need to find 'home.' It's
only when you embrace and
befriend that wilderness of pain
(such as by reaching out to
your church community for
support) that you can let it go
and count your blessings.

teachers, Dr. Norman King from the University of Windsor, helped me find meaning in my loss and gave me hope that life had purpose.

I was now able to see God not as a supreme outsider, but as a spirit that lives all around us and within us. I now see God behind a sunset, music, a child's laughter or the memories of an elderly person. And I turned to God (using prayer) to 'tune into the flow of life' – in times of hardship, or when I needed wisdom or compassion. In turn, my renewed faith helped me to become more compassionate and reach out to my larger community, so much so that I decided to make bereavement and helping others with it my lifelong career.

Pause for reflection.

Take the time to see God all around you. God is in children and grandchildren, in the beauty of a hot summer day, in the garden and in the musical voices of the birds. Once you've absorbed the beauty of the world around you, give back in the form of a smile, a loving word, or a visit to a friend in need.

As I counsel people during their final stages of life, I feel comfortable talking about their deaths and often encourage family members to do so with their loved one. For example, one of my clients, Judy (age 46), was dying of a brain tumor and was very angry with God and was alienated from her family. When I first met with her, she told me to leave her alone and not to come back. But I didn't give up on her, asking to visit her. She finally caved in and I was able to offer Judy not just advice, but a caring space – a safe place to share her fear of dying and lost dreams; to evaluate her life and affirm her value. I also offered her compassion so she could understand that there was more to life than just her

View your pain as a gift.

We all have special gifts. Use them to help others in your time of sorrow, instead of using grief to beat you down. When Steven died, I made a decision to help others in grief through counselling. I knew that God had chosen me as an instrument to help others in suffering. Today I feel a sense of sacredness when my clients trust me with their pain and invite me to walk with them on their journey.

suffering, and that this sorrow need not take away all of her meaning and hope.

Despite my strong faith, friends questioned whether we were going to have a church service for Steven because he died by suicide. Some of them questioned me either because of their own faith (they saw suicide as a sin) or because of the stigma attached to suicide. But I wasn't ashamed that Steven died this way, and I wanted to celebrate his life regardless of the cause of death. I remember responding, "my God is a loving, forgiving God and, of course, we would celebrate his life through a church service." I had come a long way from believing in the fearful, distant and dominant God image that I was taught as a child.

When my granddaughter Tate died two years later, I was shocked that I had to cope with another huge loss and I began to question my faith. I remember asking God,

"Why did this happen? Are you a real God? Why take an innocent baby? Why do this to my daughter and her husband?" I was angry with God for taking another family member's life, and I resented statements like "God has another angel now." While I didn't abandon my faith, I didn't attend church service as often, but I continued to read religious authors again with fervour. I often read the poem "Footprints" for strength and the 23rd Psalm "The Lord is my shepherd."

At the time, I was working with the dying and the bereaved, and these people gave me strength through their faith, which deepened my own faith.

It's okay to be angry with your God.

If you have a relationship with God, it is natural for you to feel anger following your loss. Pat (a client) and her family invested all of their energy into prayer when her husband was ill and did not fully prepare for his death so they were devastated when he died. She was a spiritual leader in her church and could not attend worship service until she resolved all of these feelings.

Two years later, my good friend, Nancy, died and later my husband, Rhod. When Rhod died I had the will to live but did not think I had the strength to survive. Thus began my inner spiritual journey, that is, to go through this pain and not around it. I had to discover who I was, define my purpose in life and turn my losses into gifts to help others. I didn't want to become someone who wore a coat of armour to shield me from everyday emotions. So, I chose to work through all of my unresolved grief. Grief was the hardest work that I ever had to face, but I survived it. I came to the conclusion that there were people in worse situations and was thankful for what I had in life.

Seek solace in angels.

Angels are said to be messengers from God. As a young child, I also learned that when we die, angels will come and carry us home to God. Two days before Rhod became ill, he woke me up from a deep sleep telling me he saw angels. I didn't remember his words until we were in the hospital's trauma unit and Sarah McLachlan's song "Angel" played over and over. After Rhod's death, many people gave me angel pins, statutes, etc. and I find great peace and comfort in these symbols.

RENEWING SPIRITUALITY

WHEN RHOD DIED, I EMBARKED ON A NEW SPIRITUAL
journey. I began by looking for meaning in my relationships
with my family, friends, clients, neighbours, church
community and the world around me. I took the time to
listen to my inner voice and followed that intuition. I let
myself feel my pain of loss that I had avoided when my
son Steven died. I attempted to explain the mystery of
death sometimes by saying "Steven's time on earth was
done" or "Tate is with her Uncle Steven now."

I even became more introspective, thought often about
the life after death and explored the metaphysical world. I
wondered what happens to our soul and spirit after life on
earth or if there was such a thing as reincarnation? Can
we come back again in another form of life? I needed to
make sense out of my tragedies and to find peace.

My faith and my experience with others in their final moments also gave me hope that there really was an afterlife, and that all three of my loved ones were now together with family and friends who had died earlier. For example, I viewed the afterlife through my friend Nada, who told me after her diabetic coma that she was encompassed by a serene peace, but a voice told her that she had to go back because her time to leave earth had not come yet. She was disappointed when she woke up. Just a couple of months before Rhod died, I had another epiphany that the afterlife did exist. My late friend Nancy, who had died one year earlier, came to me in a dream. In it, she held my face in her hands and she had an incredibly comforting expression of love on her face and especially in her eyes. She immediately came to mind the day Rhod died. I sensed that she knew I was going to lose him.

After Rhod died, I would often feel his comforting spirit around me. I would be sitting at my kitchen table and having a cup of tea when suddenly I would feel a light breeze around my shoulders.

My Siamese cats also gave me more reason to believe in life after death. For one year after Rhod's death, P-2 (Rhod's cat) would suddenly get up and his eyes would follow something around the room, even though nothing was there. I would speak to Rhod and say that we are okay. These were poignant spiritual moments for me.

Look for a spiritual guide.

It can be a spiritual leader, an author or well-known speaker. I read Viktor Frankl's book *Man's Search For Meaning* when I was at my lowest moments. He lived in a concentration camp under unspeakable conditions, yet he and other prisoners had fleeting moments of great joy – from the glimpse of a sunset to the treasured memories of loved ones. I would reflect on his horror and thought that if he could survive, so could I.

Turning to Spirituality

I found that my grief journey was actually a spiritual journey. I needed to go to a deep, dark place and do my painful work of healing before I could live again. Once I faced my pain, I could appreciate God's wonder around me, including my family, my relationships, my faith community, the arts and nature.

If you have 'why' questions along that journey, seek out people who will listen and not judge you as you search for answers, but realize that you many not find the answers. However, soothe your pain in one of these ways:

~ Share your story with others or listen to others with similar stories. A bereaved person sharing a similar loss will ease your loneliness and foster your self-worth.

~ Volunteer in a nursing home. Keeping a lonely senior company will give you a sense of hope by listening to his story of loss and how he coped.

~ Visit a local soup kitchen to give a couple of hours of your time and help you give meaning and purpose to life.

~ Look for peace in nature to lessen your anxiety.

~ Count the many blessings in your life to raise your hope and strength.

~ Listen to music (gospel songs), such as "Amazing Grace How
Sweet The Sound" by John Newton and "There Were Ninety
And Nine That Safely Lay" by Elizabeth Cecilia Clephane.

THE POWER OF PRAYER

It is a normal and natural reaction to turn away from your faith when
your loved one dies. You may feel anger at your loss and blame God.

But if you're feeling anger toward God, it implies you had a relationship
with him before a loved one's death, and that relationship requires
maintenance. Instead, talk (pray) to God and tell him how you feel.
Look within yourself and see what beliefs and practices sustained
you through past troubled times. Look to spiritual mentors or people
with strong faiths, such as Gandhi and Mother Theresa, who can
inspire you in your own journey. Think of the beliefs and devotions
that you admire the most. And don't forget the power prayers can
have. Some say it gives them the strength and peace to carry on.

Prayers did not bring miracles or solve my problems but they helped
me cope with them. Rather, praying gave me the strength and
courage to get through life.

∽ From My Journal ∽

February 26, 1999 – Twenty days after Rhod died. I am so confused and in shock. How can three of my loved ones die within seven years? I don't think I can survive. Will God give me the strength or is there really a God?

September 23, 1999 – I am getting though this week even though it is difficult. I have been to three funerals (clients) this week. Kay's funeral was special to me. I have known her for eight years. I am so blessed to have had these special people in my life. I was able to go to the funeral service but not graveside service. I prayed to God to give me the courage and the strength to get through and I did. I came home and went outside to nature. I am at one with God in nature.

April 3, 2000 – Jan (my good friend and volunteer) died yesterday. I visited him on Thursday and sensed that he wouldn't live through the weekend. He was very emotional and worried about leaving his wife, Rita. I assured him that she would be okay and that I would keep in touch with her. I asked him to take care of my loved ones – Rhod, Steven and Tate in the next life. He told me that he would do his best to. Wednesday evening his wife, Rita, talked to him of God and read Bible scriptures to him. During the night he found peace...I feel such humility, strength and sacredness to journey with Jan as he came to the end of his life on earth. I am strengthened by my faith in God as Jan kissed my hand goodbye.

February 6, 2001 – Second anniversary of Rhod's death. Two years seems so long and then again it seems like yesterday. Life is starting to feel good but very different. I have my moments, hours, days, but the space between the pain widens. Sometimes, I feel sorry for myself but move on and count my many blessings. At other times, I feel angry and have no answers. Only God knows! I view my life as a gift and a challenge. I have two choices...I can wallow in self-pity and be negative or lift myself up and place my energy into something healing and life-giving. I chose the latter and thank God each day and face the joy and the challenges with faith and confidence.

Strategies: Rekindle Your Spirit

Help bring new spark to your life by reconnecting with your faith and spirituality in the following ways.

1. JOIN A BIBLE STUDY GROUP.

Being a member of a Bible study group can give you hope, peace and renewed faith. Studying the Bible and sharing views with other members will give you a sense of belonging and a sense of community and help you cope with the "why" spiritual questions.

2. USE THE BENEFITS OF YOGA.

Practice yoga to lessen the stress of grieving. Its combination of breathing exercises, meditation, relaxation and stretching postures, as well as its life philosophy can help you to ride the overwhelming waves of sorrow instead of fighting them.

3. TAP INTO YOUR INTUITIVE SPIRIT.

You will be better able to cope with your grief journey if you take charge and listen to your inner voice instead of forcing yourself to do the things your gut tells you not to do.

4. **EXPERIENCE THE WONDER OF A RETREAT.**

Book a getaway retreat to evaluate your new life without your loved one. It may be a time to forgive and be forgiven. Take the time to plan in silence your future goals and dreams without any distraction or the daily chaos around you. You will come home recharged and ready to tackle the challenges of your grief journey.

5. **VOLUNTEER IN A HOSPICE SETTING.**

While the experience of visiting a hospice can give you strength and courage, wait at least a year after the death of your loved one before tackling this venture. You will need to heal before you can be an effective guide in helping someone else deal with his or her grief. The experience will give you a sense of enrichment and assist you in your loss journey and outlook on life.

RESOURCES

1. *Care of the Soul: A Guide for Cultivating Depth And Sacredness In Everyday Life* by Thomas Moore (HarperCollins Publishers, 1992)

I read this book in the first year after Rhod's death when I was searching for answers about myself. It taught me to take care of my soul in a society that Moore says is full of obsessions, addictions, violence and loss of meaning in our lives.

2. *There Are No Accidents, Synchronicity and the Stories of Our Lives* by Robert H. Hopcke (Riverhead Books, 1997)

This book tells of the unexplainable events that shape our lives. I believe that I followed my intuition to work with the dying and bereaved because it was a plan from a higher power to help me cope with my losses.

3. *Life After Life* by Raymond A. Moody, Jr., MD (Mockingbird edition, 1975; Bantam edition, 1976)

This is a classic bestseller that offers astonishing proof of life after physical death. It details the experience of more than 100 people who were clinically dead and then revived.

4. *Experiencing God All Ways And Every Day* by J. Norman King (Winston Press, 1982)

I studied this book in one of my religious studies courses after my son Steven died. My friend Norman shows us how to look and find God in key experiences, such as freedom, love, death and healing. This book gave me hope in a time of deep anguish.

5. *Siddhartha* by Hermann Hesse (New Directions Publishing Corp., 1951; Bantam edition, 1971)

This book taught me that despite my pain I could live a fulfilled and blessed life, and that my suffering was a gift to help me find wisdom and meaning in life.

CHAPTER 10

THE POWER OF
POSITIVE THINKING

I always told everyone that I was born positive; I could always see the good in bad situations. But when I was faced with the loss of my three loved ones, it was a struggle to think positive thoughts. I was on an emotional roller-coaster ride through grief and had reached the depths of despair. But I believe in the power of positive thinking and I was able to climb out of my despair.

Just the same, it's important to understand that 'positive' thinking does not guarantee a return to life the way it once was, but rather an openness to a different, but equal, life. Positivity helped me become whole again and I needed that strength to embrace a life that took a new shape. I was happy in my old life, but now I had a chance to live, love and learn in this new life.

In this chapter, I will show you how I was able to rise above sorrow, how I trained myself to turn off the negativity and switch on the positivity.

MY STORY

LIVING AGAIN

We need to grieve and mourn our loved ones. That is the price we pay when we love and our loved ones die. But by grieving forever, you are robbing yourself and your loved ones; you become one of the living dead.

I almost did. There were many days when I did not want to get out of bed in the morning. I wanted to be left alone with my pain and sorrow. Sadness and despair took a toll on my body: headaches, anxiety, digestive problems and a compromised immune system left me vulnerable to innumerable head colds, chest infections and eye infections. I lost weight and experienced extreme tiredness to the point of exhaustion. I did not have any ambition. My children had lost their father and now they were afraid they were going to lose their mother.

Luckily, there was a turning point for me. A couple of months after my husband, Rhod, died my grandson, Tristan (age 3 at the time) was visiting me for the afternoon. I was feeling very low and lethargic and trying to be a good nana although it took a lot of effort. Tristan asked me, "Nana, do you still miss Grandpa?" in a sad little voice. I was amazed at his intuition. I told him, "Yes, I miss him so much." And then we went spent an hour looking at family photos. I knew from then on that I had to maintain a positive attitude.

Of course, it was easier to wallow in self-pity and feel sorry for myself than it was to think positively. It took a lot of my energy to think and stay positive but over time I developed strategies to do so.

When the Glass is Half Full

BY TRAINING YOURSELF TO THINK POSITIVE THOUGHTS, YOU will become more aware of your needs and will be better able to express them to people supporting you. I was able to switch gears by vowing that after feeling every sad moment I would take some time to feel thankful. I made actual lists of the joys and blessings in my current life. Gradually, I was able to remain positive for longer periods of time.

That's the power of switching gears; so how do you do it? I read inspirational books, I do yoga, meditate and listen to music. Sometimes I post quotes on my refrigerator and read them daily.

Be proactive in your grief journey.

The first step in my healing process was to nurture a positive attitude. When I was positive I was able to better cope with day-to-day chores. And, I was able to seek support from my family and friends, who sent me notes and cards of encouragement, such as "yesterday is gone, tomorrow is not here and just deal with today."

Learning to say "no" will help you become more positive, especially when it means you can avoid a situation that brings you down. You know, innately, which people pick you up and which bring you down. For example, having dinner with perpetually needy, sad, high-maintenance friends is not a good idea when you're vulnerable. Even a night alone was better for me than that. I had a friend who had everything – two lovely children, financial independence, a beautiful home and loving husband. But nothing was ever good enough for her. If I commented on the beautiful blue sky, she would gloomily predict rain the next day. When I suggested she volunteer, perhaps with the elderly, she remarked that she found listening to other people's problems just "so depressing." She wasn't empathetic; she wasn't a good listener. She sucked every bit of positive energy out of me. So I avoided her. I had to put my own need for happy thoughts and feelings above anything else.

I learned how to remain positive even during the worst of times. I put on my counsellor's hat and decided to let my own grief be a lesson to others. I started a small group at my church and we took turns visiting others in the congregation that had experienced a recent loss. I continued to take courses to help me understand grief better and to help others. It was hard, at times, pulling out the sad memories, but recounting and revisiting them helped others feel less alone and helped give me new purpose. And that's a positive thing.

Find role models to inspire a positive attitude.

I think about the people that I know who, despite their disability, still maintain their positive thinking. My friend Nettie, now in her 80s, was diagnosed with multiple sclerosis when she was 30. She was in a nursing home for many years and then lobbied for an assisted living residence and succeeded. She lived independently and always accepted her condition despite her deteriorating health. She even knitted socks, gloves and scarves for the less fortunate people.

Banishing Negative Thoughts

I CONTINUED TO KEEP NEGATIVE THOUGHTS IN CHECK BY counting my blessings. At times, I did think negative thoughts, but I did not allow these thoughts to control me. I allowed myself some time to be negative and then I told myself to get over it because I had so many good things in my life.

Setting goals also helps to focus the mind in the present and help you envision a life in the future. I set goals throughout my life. Despite getting married when I was a teenager and having three young children, I always had a dream of going to university. I decided to set a goal of accomplishing this in the '80s. I was doing part-time studies, working full time and raising a family, but I graduated in 1993 as planned.

When my loved ones died, I used the same discipline when setting new goals. I vowed I would take early retirement from the Victorian Order of Nurses, start my small business (I'm actually working full time and loving it!) and write a book. Well, here's the book, and my small business is successful.

It's important to set goals early. In the beginning, your goal may be just getting through the day, but gradually, you can start setting longer-term goals. I set a long-term goal of opening a private practice in grief counselling in 2002; then I set about breaking it down into small steps. And then I determined a deadline for each step.

So set a mission statement (I will put my grief to good use, was mine), establish a long-term goal and then start by taking baby steps. Before long, you'll find yourself in a happier place.

~ From My Journal ~

September 20, 1999 – Dear Lord, thank you for giving me the strength to get through each day. Thank you for giving me the determination and courage to journey in my grief throughout this roller-coaster ride. Thank you for blessing me with such a wonderful family and loving friends whose support and prayers I need and cherish. Thank you for allowing me to see the beauty of nature, the gift of music and the many blessings I receive each day. Thank you for the ability to see that there are people in worse positions. Thank you for my positive attitude, my sense of humour and, most of all, my reasonably good health. Amen

---

August 25, 2001 – Nine years today since Steven died and 18 months since Rhod died. It is a bittersweet day and I'm reliving memories of both of my loved ones. But I also sense an awakening of my mind, body and soul. I have a need to smell the flowers, listen to the birds sing and still my trembling heart.

August 9, 2003 – It's true...strangers are friends that we haven't yet met. I look forward to meeting new friends and today I met a special friend and his name was Michael. We shared special moments, sad moments and life experiences. We shared our losses and our joys. Three hours disappeared in a moment on that plane ride. Life is good. I am blessed.

DESPAIR SIGNALS

I found it difficult to think about positive things for the first couple of months, but over time, I motivated myself to think positive things. However, if you find that you can't function with daily activities you may need intervention. When the husband of one of my friends died, she could not bathe or feed herself for two months, just like an infant. Another friend abused alcohol and drugs and indulged in risky sexual behaviour to attempt to dull the pain of loss. It didn't work; worse, as a result of his promiscuity, he was estranged from his family and friends. It was only when he attempted suicide that he sought help from a therapist for unresolved grief.

If you find yourself incapacitated, or are having suicidal thoughts, seek help from your family doctor or therapist.

NOTE: *It is very important that you consult with your family doctor if you were taking medications before the death of your loved one and plan to discontinue them.*

Strategies: Practice Pick-Me-Ups

The death of a loved one can make us feel like there's nothing left in life worth living. But you can work through this tragedy and you'll see that there's still a lot more living to do. Here are some ways to view life more positively.

1. TAKE A BREAK FROM YOUR GRIEF AND DESPAIR.

Allow yourself time each day to think positive thoughts. When I got up in the morning I sat at my kitchen table with a cup of tea and wrote down why I should feel positive and why I should feel negative. In the beginning of my journey the negatives overpowered the positives, but as time went on, the positives overtook the negatives.

2. HANG OUT WITH CHILDREN.

Children make us feel positive; they bring out our inner child. My grandchildren were great for my grieving process – we played games, went to the park and they made me laugh. If you don't have any children or grandchildren, volunteer at the local school or babysit for a neighbour or a friend.

3. MAKE BREAD.

Throw away your bread maker and make bread with your hands. There is something wonderful about having your hands in the dough and creating a masterpiece that tastes so yummy. I learned to make bread as a teenager and loved to watch the bread rise and then smell its aroma when baking. I get rid of my frustrations while kneading and punching the dough.

4. JOIN AN ART CLASS.

There is something positive about creating an object with your imagination and your hands. Moulding clay or working with paints is very uplifting to your mind and spirit. We have to work with our grief, like a piece of clay, moulding it and shaping it into something beautiful.

5. PRACTICE POSITIVE VISUALIZATION.

You might think it's easy to visualize yourself in positive situations, but perfecting the technique takes practice. What worked for me was to lie down with my eyes closed, picturing myself on a beach with the warm sun caressing my body and the waves lapping at my toes. The beach resonates with me, but a different, peaceful place may be better for you. Is there a cherished childhood vacation destination that you can visualize?

6. ENJOY THE COMPANY OF THE ELDERLY.

The elderly have so much wisdom and experience they can share with you. If you don't have an elderly friend, seek out a neighbour or consider volunteering with a seniors' association in your community. You can provide a lonely senior with a much-needed visit and gain tremendous insight on your grief journey.

7. MAKE PLANS TO ENJOY LIFE AGAIN.

Try to imagine what your life will be like five years after the death of your loved one. Set some short- and long-term goals. Travel? A course? A new pet? Let your own interests lead you. Imagine yourself growing through your grief process and not becoming bitter.

RESOURCES

1. *The Power of Positive Thinking* by Norman Vincent Peale (Fawcett Columbine Book, Ballantine Books, 1963)

I read this book many years ago and gained much knowledge and understanding of the power of positive thinking.

2. *Counting My Blessings: A Journal of Things to be Thankful For* by Artworks International, Inc.

A daily gratitude journal given to me by my good friend Renata, who suffered many losses herself and knew that this tool would help me stay positive.

3. *Manifest your Destiny: The Nine Spiritual Principles For Getting Everything You Want* by Wayne W. Dyer (HarperCollins Publishers, 1977)

I read this book to inspire my confidence and to set future goals and maintain a positive attitude. I especially centred on the "ninth principle:" Do you complain, find fault, or take for granted more often than you appreciate your life?

RESOURCES FOR BEREAVED PEOPLE

Bereaved Families of Ontario

293 Wellington St. N., Ste. 118
Hamilton, ON L84 8E7
Tel: (905) 318-0070
Fax: (905) 318-9181
www.bereavedfamilies.net

Bereavement Magazine

Bereavement Publishing Inc.
4765 North Carefree Circle
Colorado Springs, CO 80917-2118
Toll free: 1-888-604-HOPE (4673)
Fax: (719) 573-4676
www.bereavementmag.com

Bereavement Ontario Network

P.O. Box 24038
London, ON N6H 5C4
Tel: (519) 474-7700
Fax: (519) 473-7721
www.BereavementOntarioNetwork.ca

Canadian Centre for Bereavement Education and Grief Counselling

80 Carlton St., Ste. 10
Toronto, ON M5B 1L6
Tel: (416) 926-0905

Canadian Palliative Care Association

Annex B, Saint-Vincent Hospital
60 Cambridge St. North
Ottawa, ON K1R 7A5
Tel: (613) 241-3663 Ext. 227
Toll free: 1-800-668-2785
Hospice Palliative Care Info Line:
1-877-203-4636
www.cpca.net

The Center For Loss and Life Transition

3735 Broken Bow Rd.
Fort Collins, CO 80526
Tel: (970) 226-6050
Fax: 1-800-922-6051
www.centerforloss.com

Compassion Books

477 Hannah Branch,
Burnsville, NC 28714
Tel: (828) 675-5909
Fax: (828) 675-9687
www.compassionbooks.com

The Compassionate Friends, Inc.

P.O. Box 3696
Oak Brook, IL 60522-3696
Toll free: 1-877-969-0010
Tel: (630) 990-0010
Fax: (630) 990-0246
www.compassionatefriends.org

Coping Centre

1740 Blair Rd.
Cambridge, ON N3H 4R8
Toll free: 1-877-554-4498
Tel: (519) 650-0852
Fax: (519) 650-1949
www.griefsupport.cc

The Funeral Service Association of Canada

6-14845 Yonge St., Ste. 192
Aurora, ON L4G 6H8
Tel: (905) 841-7779
Toll free: 1-866-841-7777
Fax: (905) 841-0992
www.fsac.ca

Genesis Bereavement Resources

P.O. Box 184
Warkworth, ON K0K 3K0
Tel: (705) 924-2458
Toll free: 1-866-924-2458
Fax: (705) 924-1709
www.genesis-resources.com

Grief Recovery Institute — Canada

RR# 1, St. Williams, ON N0E 1P0
Tel: (519) 586-8825
Fax: (519) 586-8826
www.grief-recovery.com

In-Sight Books

P.O. Box 42467
Oklahoma City, OK 73123
Tel: (405) 810-9501
Toll free: 1-800-658-9262
Fax: (405) 810-9504
www.insightbooks.com
Through the company's training arm, In-Sight Institute, founder Doug Manning also offers Funeral Celebrant Training.

Ontario Palliative Care Association

194 Eagle St.
Newmarket, ON L3Y 1J6
Tel: (905) 954-0938
Toll free: 1-888-379-6666
Fax: (905) 954-0939
www.ontariopalliativecare.org

Seniors Canada On-line

It has a special section called "End of Life," which lists many resources for those facing loss.
www.seniors.gc.ca

READER FEEDBACK

How Did This Book Affect Your Grief Journey?
I Want To Hear From You.

Share your stories and experiences of loss with me. I will make every possible effort to respond with a personal note. Please write to:

Audrey Stringer
c/o A String of Hope Inc.
P.O. Box 22037
Sarnia, ON
N7S 6J4

Or contact me via e-mail at: astringofhope@sympatico.ca

ORDER FORM

Check your local bookstore for *Get Over It!* or order here.

ORDER BY:

TELEPHONE: (519) 383-0161
E-MAIL: astringofhope@sympatico.ca
MAIL: Audrey Stringer, c/o A String of Hope Inc.,
P.O. Box 22037, Sarnia, ON N7S 6J4

PRICE: $19.95 CAN*; $17.95 US
(Please note that shipping and handling costs are extra)

*Canadian residents add 7% G.S.T.
Please make cheques payable to:
A String of Hope Inc.

Ask about discount orders on quantity purchases for your organization.